LONDON
FOLK
TALES

LONDON
FOLK TALES

HELEN EAST

*with Alex Yedigaroff
and Xanthe Gresham*

First published 2012

The History Press
The Mill, Brimscombe Port
Stroud, Gloucestershire, GL5 2QG
www.thehistorypress.co.uk

British Library Cataloguing in Publication Data.
A catalogue record for this book is available from the British Library.

ISBN 978 0 7524 6185 4

Typesetting and origination by The History Press
Printed in Great Britain

CONTENTS

Illustration of stained-glass window from All Hallows by the Tower; reproduced with permission of the Vicar. The wonderful church of All Hallows, with its Undercroft Museum, spans the centuries from Roman times to present-day London.

FOREWORD

The making of books about London continues unabated, but in the welter of information, comment and tourist-targeted coffee-table picture books, there are never enough collections of tales and legends – stories told by and for real Londoners.

Helen East has pulled together a delightful collection of folk stories, old and new, from across the Greater London area, presenting some well-known tales with others which will be completely new to most readers. The range of subjects and styles is wide, and only in a book from London can Boudicca and Dick Whittington rub shoulders with the Lambeth Pedlar and a strangely touching story of a deceased first wife's spirit making life uncomfortable for an ordinary widowed woman from Streatham.

Folk tales and legends can be studied, classified, analysed, pulled apart and debunked, but whatever indignities they are put through they survive by being told and re-told – by professional storytellers and ordinary folk, and in books such as this.

Steve Roud, 2012

ACKNOWLEDGEMENTS

Huge thanks to the many people who told me stories, especially Joan Cottle, Gertie, Debbie Guneratne, Brian Hayden, Wally Saunders, Liz Thompson and Geoff Wilson.

Much gratitude to Xanthe Gresham who wrote one (Boudicca).

Thanks also to: The vicar of All Hallows by the Tower, sculptor Luke Morgan and The Chapter of Southwark Cathedral for permission to reproduce artifacts as illusrations.

The Folklore Society, Borough, Guildhall, Museum of London and British Libraries

FLS members: Caroline Oates, Steve Roud, Jeremy Hart and Paul Cowdell

Friends and family: Amy, Alex, Isabel, Roger and above all Rick for support.

And Postman Park – for reminders of unsung heroes, and legends of tomorrow.

Text by Helen East. Illustrations/photographs by Alex Yedigaroff (who has been taking photos ever since he was old enough to hold a camera).

Introduction

London Legends, Folk Tales and Fibs

These stories, ordered roughly chronologically, are as true as I stand here before you. Which is to say that they are not. Yet, in a way, they are too. Just as I may be represented by my words without literally being there, so these stories are full of truths of sorts. Some are wound in and out of history, but embroidered like the Bayeux tapestry; some are fictions hooked onto historical events or physical remains; and some are told to me as true by people who I have every reason to believe, despite them being about things which I have never seen. Then there are those like folk tales, which are true in their depiction of people's behaviour and emotion, if not in the trappings of the tale that they dress in. And at least one is a porky pie.

Londoners love playing with words. And possibilities increase with the more languages that join the mix. My grandfather, George – although it transpired when he died that that wasn't his name after all – was born in Rotherhithe, and he claimed he'd been in earshot of Bow Bells. Hence he was technically cockney, which some say is an egg laid by a cockerel and others a Londoner with a liking for doggerel. He'd tantalise me with words of double meaning and

stories that went nowhere, like the one about the 'three holes in the ground'. All I got was, 'well, well, well'.

He also told true tales. He was at the theatre the night Queen Victoria died. The show stopped, they went outside – and London was alive. Shops and stalls all candlelit, selling black bands and ties. 'How did traders get ready so quick?'

'Word runs down the street.'

Or in King Edward's time, the newspaper scam that had every child, woman and man mucky as mudlarks digging the river beach at South Bermondsey for 'hidden money'.

'Are you sure it's true?' he'd asked.

'Yes! The newspaper gives clues.'

'How do you know they're right?'

'Look – it's down in black and white.'

'Silly,' I said.

'Maybe,' he smiled, 'but don't believe and don't look – you certainly won't find it.'

His stories made me reach across the centuries and touch another time. I hope these will do the same for you. Don't just believe them because you read them. Check the notes at the end to help unravel facts from fibs.

I saw a pack of cards gnawing on a bone
I saw a dog sitting on England's throne
I saw the Queen shut up in a box
I saw a shilling talking to a fox
I saw a man blown round London streets all night
I saw leaves reading a book by candlelight
I saw a girl explain how it could be true
I saw these sights and so perhaps might you.

Helen East, 2012

1

ALBA TO BRUTUS

Before before, when the world was raw, and all things elemental, the earth gave birth to many monstrous creatures. Amongst them was a race of giants. It is from them, some people say, that mankind came.

Be that as it may, the giants fitted in as best they could. A few grew taller, others smaller; they bred, and just as naturally they spread. Some settled and then claimed the land; while some battled and renamed the land. Some borders changed and yet old names remained. Europe was one.

Time passed. Rulers, races and regimes rose and were deposed. Then came a leader of a great dynasty. But amongst his countless children he had thirty-three daughters who brought him no pleasure whatsoever. They were strong and self-willed, they were steadfast and stubborn – even his orders were sometimes ignored. And Alba, the eldest, was worst of them all.

In a fury, he parted them, locked them all up, and forced them to marry – even those far too young. He found them hard husbands who were heavy handed and harsh-tongued. Men who kept women well under their thumb. But the new brides resisted. The worse they were treated, the stronger they grew. They met with their sisters in secret, and plotted. And one night at a signal from Alba, they acted. All poisoned their husbands – each in their own way.

By the time they were caught and condemned for this crime, it was clear that each one of them carried a child. Not wanting the blame for destroying the seed, their father had all of them put out to sea. He gave them a ship, but no sails and no oars, no rudder, no water and no food at all. No help and no hope, they still sang as they went, and the moon held them tight in her light, like a net.

They drifted without aim for days and days, until they came to the place beyond the waves, the lost land to the west, at the back of the north wind. Cold, fog-smothered cliffs cut sharp into the water. There the ship ran aground, and out stepped the thirty-three daughters.

And from those women came the future of that island, which they called Albion after their sister, and they peopled it with the children that they carried. Alba became the Queen, and she gave birth to a monstrous child, ferocious as his father. But yet she loved him, and she nursed him, and she named him Gogmagog.

Meanwhile across the seas, on southern winds, in warmer waters, a bloody battle brewed and broke. The Trojans and the Greeks turned friends to foes and wives to widows, all for the sake of honour and a single woman – Helen. All know of that story, and of the endless siege, broken by the wooden horse of Ulysses.

When the Trojans had been tricked and their city had been sacked, many died, but some survived. Amongst the ones that did, who fled across the sea to safer lands, was a man named Aeneas; and with him was his son. They took a piece of stone from the walls of Troy, so the memory of its glory should not be wholly lost.

The years passed. New roots grew. The son was married and his wife gave birth. But all the while she struggled, they could hear the Moirae muttering the destiny of the child to come:

This thread of fate winds dark and light.
For mother and father he brings death.
In lands behind the north wind's breath
He leads a whole new nation into life.

Well the birth was hard and the boy was big, and the mother died from the labour. So that was the first warning come true.

They called the boy Brutus, and he grew swiftly. His father was always his closest companion. But when he was ten years old, the two went hunting and Brutus fired an arrow too much into the wind. It turned in the air and fell straight back, and hit his father in the heart. So that was the second threat proved, too.

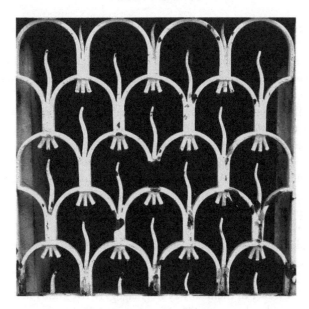

Then his grandfather Aeneas decided it was time for him to go on his way; to test the truth of the third prophecy. He gave him a boat, with silver sails, and the boy chose companions to travel with him, and took the piece of stone from Troy also.

Away they went as the winds took them, with the land but a shadow on the horizon.

They sailed for days and for weeks and for years until they were weather-beaten and hardened by their travels. And many adventures they had along the way. But at last they came to a leg of land that jutted out, with nothing beyond but the sea.

There was a harbour town there where they landed, and the lord of the land came out to meet them. When Brutus told him of their quest he begged them to stay with him and rest.

'And perhaps you will wish to stop here, where it is safe,' he said. 'For the land you seek, at the back of the north wind, is the place that we call Death. Beyond the grey cold sea, beyond all life that we know.'

But Brutus said no – he was following his Fate, and had to see if the words he had heard were true.

Then the lord sighed and nodded his head. 'There are some in this town,' he said, 'who are strong, adventurous and young, and would wish to travel with you if you would let them come. And amongst them is my son. Like you, he is destined for more than he will find here, though I have always wanted him to stay.'

Then Brutus was happy, and they met with the young men of the town. And of those that joined them, the strongest and the tallest and the most eager of them all was Corineus, the son of the old lord. He was a giant of a man, and an adventurer after Brutus' own heart. In no time they were friends, and Corineus became the second in command. And now they were ready to go on.

Together they travelled; teeth into the north wind and with every day it got colder and darker, and the waves rose higher and wilder. Until, at last, they came to tall white cliffs that seemed to reach from the sea to the sky. And when they landed they saw that it was a place of giants.

The leader of them all was Gogmagog, twelve cubits high, as hard and harsh as rock. When he saw them climbing up towards him, he laughed with all the force of a storm wind. 'Come all at once against me,' he cried, 'and I will still destroy you with one blow!'

Then Corineus stepped forward and begged Brutus for a chance to prove his strength alone. And when the right was given him, he turned towards great Gogmagog and challenged him.

At once the giant caught him in his arms, and gave Corineus a hug so terrible it broke three of his ribs. But the young hero tore himself away, and then, enraged, ran head to belly, knocking him so hard that Gogmagog fell back and smashed his head against the stony ground. Yet, in a moment he was up again as if he'd merely paused to rest in bed. And so the fighting went, Gogmagog with ever-increasing strength at every fall, until, at last, Corineus, forced down onto his knees, pulled out his sword, and with both hands swung it round. He sliced the giant through, so he was cut in two. Both halves fell down upon the earth, but as they lay, the mangled limbs began to move and creep to meet their other parts, and to grow together into one again.

'How can this be, against all nature's laws?' Corineus cried.

'But it is not,' the giant replied. 'The Earth herself is my great grandmother. In her hold, I will grow whole. She will never see me suffer.'

Then Corineus understood that he would never win by fighting man to man as he had always done. But in that instant too, he knew what he must do. Catching Gogmagog by surprise, he snatched him up before his wounds had time to fully heal, and heaving him over his shoulder, held him up as high as he could. The giant tried to struggle, but, distanced from the ground, he was weakening fast.

Then, balancing his burden as best he could, Corineus turned and ran along a jagged splinter of land that reached far out into the sea. At its sharp tip he caught his breath, and then hurled great Gogmagog over the cliff's edge, plunging him headlong from that great height into the angry water. Down into the foam he fell, far beyond the Earth's soft touch, sinking deep into the ocean, subject to the Sea's dominion. And when his body tore upon the ocean floor, the blood came bubbling forth and lay like sunset froth upon the waves, staining the sea, sand, cliffs and land.

To this day, the earth along that shore is still rich red. And the high point, where Gogmagog fell, is called 'Langoemagog'. As for that long leg of land touching the sea to the south and the west, it became known as Cornwall, after Corineus, who settled there as governor.

But Brutus and the rest of his men went on their way, towards the setting sun. After some days they found a stream that trickled from a high-pointed hill. They followed this until it widened into a great river, and flowed at last towards the east and into the sea. But before it came to that, there was a place where it was possible to ford the river, and there was good solid ground rising up on the northern side. There they stopped to rest, and Brutus said this was the place to build a settlement.

When they had done that, he marked all around to show the extent of the place, and put up defences where it was needed, and then made an entrance way to come in by. On either side of that they made two great figures, as guardians of the gate, and they were known as Corineus and Gogmagog – in memory of the two great fighters, and the battle between them to win the land of Albion.

And finally Brutus took his talisman, the great stone brought by Aeneas from Troy, and he set it in the centre of the new settlement. Then they named it after the old city, 'Troynovante' or New Troy, and Brutus told them that one day it would become a great city too, and the heart of the whole island.

They say that Brutus renamed the island, and it was known from then as Britain, after him, and the race that he founded were called the Brits, or Britons. As for his settlement, it grew as he had prophesised, into a city that eclipsed even Troy in fame; only the name changed again and again until it became known as London.

Some say all of this is nothing but a tale. Yet the Stone of Brutus continues to stands here, and can be seen still within London's city walls. And the giant guardians are remembered too, although their effigies have had to be remoulded time and again, and their looks and then their names have altered too. Corineus eventually slipped from public memory, and Gogmagog was then split into two. So the images carved in medieval times, guarding the gates of the London Guildhall, or the statues seen today standing in the hallway there, and paraded through the London streets in each Lord Mayor's show, are now known as brother giants, Gog and Magog, the ancient defenders of the realm.

2

BRAN THE BLESSED

As night follows day, and light and dark are two halves of the same circle, so was King Bran, the Raven, to his sister Branwen, the White One. Bran the Blessed was king of these isles, a giant of a man, and the last of the great race. Tall as an oak, he could wade halfway across the sea to Ireland in the west, without the need of a boat.

It was to that country he was looking now, and the royal ships arriving from there; for he was hoping that a match between his sister and the king of that land, Matholwch, would bring a union of affection, and a settled peace to them all.

So it seemed to prove, for when the bridal pair met together, in the palace of Harlech, there was a flame of liking lit between them, which promised to grow into love.

But Bran and Branwen had two half-brothers by another father, who were in every way the opposite of each other. Nisien was serene, a listener and peacemaker, while his brother Efnisien was resentful and rash, and the centre of endless disputes.

Because of this Bran decided not to invite Efnisien to the wedding feast. That was his first and his worst mistake – for the circle was broken and Efnisien was insulted. And so, when his chance came, he sowed the seeds of conflict. On the morning of the wedding, he went to the royal stables where the King of Ireland's beautiful horses were steaming and stamping all ready to ride out with their new friends, the horses of the Isles of Britain.

He went to each of the horses, the finest steeds of Ireland, the guests of his brother, the king, and cut off each and every one of their tails, their ears and their lips.

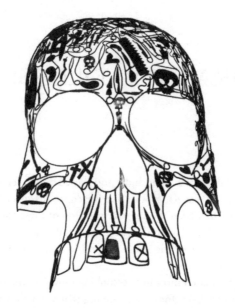

When Matholwch saw how his horses had been maimed, he was beside himself with grief and rage. Bran gave him equal horses from his own stables, and ten times the value of the animals in gifts of incomparable riches and magical power, which the King of Ireland accepted as compensation for the deed, but the insult cut so deep into the hearts of the Irish, it was never to be healed.

This was the cause of the wars to come. Although the wedding went ahead, and Branwen went with her new husband home to Ireland, and within a year bore him a son and heir, the harm done to the horses festered in the mind of the Irish people. And at last they rose up, and demanded that the insult be repaid.

And so Branwen, the Queen, was stripped of all her honours. Her son was taken from her and she herself was sent down to the kitchens to be the maid of all work, the lowest of the low. And every day the cook, all greasy from his work, would box her ears until her whole head rang and she could scarcely hear. All this she endured without a word, in secret sorrow, all alone.

Three years passed in this way, and never a whisper of it was leaked over the sea to Britain. Then one morning a starling chick on its first flight fell down and broke its wing. Branwen saw it and secretly nursed it back to health. Day by day she talked to it, and told it all her troubles, until it had listened so long that the bird itself learned how to speak her tongue. And then she sent it home to tell her tale to her brother Bran.

That was how the war began between those islands and between those men. And when it was done, such were the losses on both sides that there was barely anyone left alive – even Bran himself was dying on the battlefield. So he told the seven men who still survived to cut off his great head and carry it back home, and all around his isles. He promised them that whilst they went, his eyes would stay alive to see, his ears to hear, and his mouth to speak. And when the time came that the life and soul went from him, he told them to take him eastwards, to 'Gwynfryn', the white hill, and bury him.

Then Branwen's heart burst with the sorrow of it all, and the sense that she was the cause. But the head of Bran continued to live for all the time that it was carried on its journey home, and for those seven years of pilgrimage around his lands. And throughout this time he told his men stories and sang them songs of old, and gave such wise advice that he consoled them all. Those seven years seemed to them no more than seven hours, such was the good company they had together – all thoughts of troubles gone.

Then the moment came when the doors were opened to the memory of all that they had lost, and the head of Bran fell silent, and the flesh began to rot. They carried it then towards the east, over the hills, and across the flatter lands, following a river that grew ever wider until it poured out into the eastern sea. But before it came to that, there was a settlement on the northern side of the river, beside a white hill, and they knew they had come to Gwynfryn, and they buried the head there, with his face towards the east.

They say that settlement was once called Troynovant, and then had many names, of which London is the latest. And upon that white hill a White Tower was built, and other towers and defences grew around it to make the Tower of London as we know it today.

It was said, too, that Bran's head would keep this island safe from all invasion, so long as it remained in that place. Some claim

Arthur moved it, when he was king at Camelot, but others say that he did not, and that we stay, to this day, protected by its power.

Either way, we can rest assured that if Britain is not saved by his remains, then it will be by symbolic representations of the ancient king.

For 'Bran' is 'Raven' by another name, and those black birds of wisdom have been at the Tower of London for as long as the tale has been told, further back than any can remember. Indeed, King Charles II, who knew the legend well, made a royal decree that a minimum of six ravens must be kept at the tower at all times. Nowadays they are looked after by a special official, the Yeomen Warder Ravenmaster. Amongst other things, he attends to clipping their wings, which I am told is for their own benefit, as opposed to an attempt to prevent our royal winged defenders from trying to fly away.

3

BOUDICCA

There are plenty of stars in London but they usually stay at the Ritz and dine at The Ivy. The real stars, the kind that twinkle, the ones we wish on, are hidden behind a layer of smog. But Londoners always see the moon. She does not forget us.

Civilisations are like the moon. They begin no bigger than a thumbnail in a vast sky, and then become an apple of light as big as a cartwheel, and then decay to a rind and go back into the dark. Occasionally a human being becomes as famous as a civilisation and every time we tell their story, they shine as bright as a moon.

Boudicca, Queen of the Iceni, ruled in the east of England. She was very rich. She was rich because she was a queen, she was rich because she was a mother, but most of all she was rich in herself. She was big – about 6ft tall – with legs as strong as the hind legs of a hare, and arms as free as the strong, beating wings of the sacred geese and swans that strutted and pecked between her many dwellings. Her laugh was as deep and low as a wood pigeon cooing over its eggs. At first glance, Boudicca's eyes flashed like green water through the trees, but on second glance, you might notice flecks of brown in the green, like tough pebbles holding back the skip of the river.

Like the black crow of the dark forest, its eyes bright but hooded, Boudicca didn't know what was coming her way. Like a root that curls round an obstacle and continues to thrive, she fancied she could subsist alongside the Romans. Her husband tolerated them and she followed his lead. They made her laugh, with their hard hats and hard lines, their regiments and their rules. It was ludicrous the way they tried to untangle the gorse and the bramble, pave over

the marshes and fight the wind and the river. Didn't they know how much easier it was just to watch how the water bubbled up from the depths of the lake, and then follow its curves and patterns like a fish? Each to his own, but Boudicca vowed she would never be a Roman. She would follow the signs of the seasons, the path of the stars and the voice inside herself.

When her husband died, he left half of his wealth to the Romans, and the rest to his family. It didn't occur to Boudicca that anyone would dare defy his wishes, but she was wrong.

Early one morning, the sun was still behind the mountains, the pigs were grunting and the geese were padding their yellow feet in the yard and Boudicca was fast asleep with her daughters. She was lying on her back, her arms and legs spread wide; a daughter on each side, their soft hair like copper feathers brushing her arms. Had her eyes been open, she might have seen the blade of a knife split the heavy skins acting as a door, but it wasn't until boots kicked through the soft carpets to the dust of the floor, that she finally opened them. By then it was too late. A multitude of calloused hands grabbed at her and she was dragged away from her daughters, like a hen separated from her chicks. She fought back, howling, beating with her strong legs and swift arms, but she was utterly outnumbered.

Boudicca was strapped to a pole and beaten, but no matter how hard the rods bit into her back she was always conscious of the cries of her daughters, like fox cubs screeching in the night, as they were dragged through the dust by mauling soldiers who broke their soft skin and tore their bright hair. And when she was finally released from the pole, she crawled through the dung of the yard to where her daughters had been thrown onto the stones like rich scraps from a banquet table. Shivering in each other's arms, they watched the Roman robbers stack their possessions onto carts – their torques, armbands, bracelets of gold, hides, fleeces, finely woven cloth, bowls, benches, tables of oak and mirrors of bronze. Helplessly they looked on as the Romans speared Boudicca's holy birds, spit the pigs, tethered the cattle and rode all of it away.

And so the warp pole of war between the Romans and Britons was slammed into the ground as Boudicca planned her revenge, crafted as carefully as a carpet. First the beams of the loom had to be straightened; Boudicca and her daughters healed themselves to full strength. Then the tying and tightening of the warp strings commenced; so they amassed followers, going from dwelling to dwelling, tribe to tribe and rousing them to commit to the war cloth. And then the weaving of the decorative threads began, as the women and men prepared their bodies and their boasts, cursing the Romans, spitting oaths in an out of each other's hearts like blood-red wool, like night-black thread:

If Rome is an eagle then we are the lions.
If Rome is a wolf then we are the bears.
If Rome is a road then we are the river
If Rome is a rock then we are the ice.

An ever-expanding carpet of warriors gathered. Their hair bristled, limed white and streaked with crimson; their skin writhed with blue tattoos of snakes and leaves. They jostled and joked with each other, juggling with spears or crossing their swords and dancing between the points, waiting for an omen to guide them.

A murder of black crows flew up from the echoing forest and Boudicca mounted her chariot. She stood tall in newly crafted blue and red tartan, a freshly forged golden torque heavy round her neck, her untamed hair catching the rays of the morning sun. She raised her arms towards it, feeling its beams flowing into her blood until it fizzed like liquid gold. One hundred and twenty thousand warriors exhaled with one breath as she spoke, her voice low and rhythmic like wind blowing down from the hills.

'Andraste, Goddess of Victory, I am speaking to you woman to woman. You know we will win this battle, I know we will win this battle, now show my people we will win this battle!'

And she pulled out from underneath her thick cloak, a hare. She held it by its enormous ears with one hand and while her other hand steadied its great, thumping hind legs, she began to chant in its ear. The crowd inhaled and listened with the holy hare – the hare that runs like the river, spawns like the salmon, and boxes like the bear. Then they swelled out Boudicca's chant with their own voices, until they were one with the hare, and the hare was one with them.

'Tell me,' said Boudicca – pitching her voice just above theirs, 'if she runs to the right will we win or lose?'

'We will lose!' they crooned.

'If she runs to the left will we lose or win?'

'We will win!'

'Then let her begin!'

And Boudicca stepped smoothly down from her wicker chariot and lightly placed the hare on the ground. Raising her front paws and sniffing the air, the hare held the little stage of green grass for a moment, and then dropped her front legs and ran straight through the parting wave of warriors, until she veered surely and swiftly to the left, disappearing into the folds of the forest. Then the army of warriors cheered, and surged ahead to take their first town, Camilodnum, the Colchester of today.

The inhabitants were caught by surprise. Most of them were retired Roman soldiers whose muscles had turned to fat and whose heroic exploits had turned into stories. Some were sitting in warm taverns, the click of a knucklebone here, the chink of a marble there; others were strolling to the baths or the temple, but the swishes of their robes were silenced by cries that raised the hairs on their scarred arms. There was no time to reach for their rusty weapons; they were cut, crucified, hanged and hacked as their statues crashed down around them along with their temples, arenas and squares and Boudicca's war cloth smothered them with its black and red threads.

'I spit on your Emperor God!' cursed Boudicca. 'Under this stone are the bones of the Trinovantes, our people. Your stones have silenced the gods of earth, air and water – the only voice left is fire!'

The city was torched.

On the other side of the country, the Roman Governor, General Seutonius, was otherwise engaged. This was a man who had put down rebellions for twenty years, driven his troops through icy rivers, tramped over the Atlas Mountains and marched through the burning deserts of the Sahara; all in the name of Rome. He had cauterised all sentiment, all personal interest had been erased in his worship of the Empire.

When he heard of Boudicca's uprising, and the hysterical accounts of her ever-expanding army advancing on Londinium, he marched his men 250 miles to reach the city well before she got there. Seutonius never wasted time. He needed to perform a risk assessment.

Londinium was in its infancy then; approximately thirty acres on the north side of the river, spread across rising ground above a white hillock. Although it had its fair share of solid traders of fresh produce, skins and ironware, most of its inhabitants were more like bankers, dealing in virtual exchanges and living in timber-framed houses with thatched roofs, wooden floors and fine furniture that sported Mediterranean coloured glass and Samian pottery. Their cellars were stocked with notable wines and when they were not passing gold from palm to palm, they spent their days talking, listening to music and discussing poetry and art.

Seutonius took in their pasty skins and trembling lips and couldn't help making a comparison to his soldiers – the kind of men that back in Rome would have been blacksmiths or butchers; men made of muscle and sinew; builders of bridges and roads and houses; broad of chest from carrying heavy kit; strong in the arm from working out with swords and spears; and thick in the thigh from marching 25 miles a day. Their only music was marching songs, their only object of contemplation the golden eagle of their standard and the lightning flashes upon their shields.

A vertical line of concentration crossed the horizontal lines of General Seutonius' craggy forehead as he retired to assemble the facts. He made quick diagrams of Boudicca's attacks, only speaking to call for maps, and it wasn't long before he narrowed his eyes, clicked his jaw, cracked his knuckles and came to the conclusion that Londinium must fend for itself – he simply didn't have enough men to win against Boudicca.

As he rode out of Londinium with his troops, the old and young, women and children all clung to his legs but he shook them off with precise flicks, keeping his eyes on the distant horizon. 'Those that can, must run,' he repeated 'those with means must use the river, and as for the rest of you – help is just not cost-effective, toughen up.'

As Boudicca's ever-ecstatic host approached London, they strung more strings on the loom of war, gathering more warriors to the fight, Boudicca whipping them into frenzy as they went. 'Iceni! Iceni! Trinovantes! Corvoni! Brigantes! I am a woman, a woman as you are women, as you are men. I am a woman whose daughters were violated, whose back was beaten, whose wealth was stolen. Fight! Don't submit to the scythe of these Roman bandits!'

Her chariot was spattered with blood. Around the necks of her horses were garlanded the heads of Romans – dipped in cedar oil, until they glistened like uprooted bulbs looking for soil. A tsunami roared in her ears, a volcano erupted in her heart, while her will grew wings and danced on the tips of the spears of her people, like a crow with many beaks. In their excitement, warriors leaped on, and from, their speeding chariots, spinning their swords and performing feats for their families to applaud. Women whirled their arms like spinning wheels, their necks bulged, and their legs kicked as they slaughtered alongside their menfolk.

The day belonged to Boudicca, and her people torched the city. The Queen of the Iceni blazed like a full moon. Andraste had made her a goddess for a moment. But for the inhabitants of London, that goddess was a great black crow spreading the war cloth of her wings over the face of their moon. To this day, London remembers Boudicca in her entrails – London has a layer of red earth 4m below her surface, not from the bloodshed, but from the oxidised iron of the fire that blazed at 1,000 degrees.

And while London was blazing, General Seutonius pared his fingernails and considered the difference between the Romans and the Britons. His men were trained and properly armed. Every Roman soldier had a helmet, armour, a studded belt and studded sandals, whereas the Britons fought naked or in cotton trousers. They were farmers and family men as well as fighters and only a few had chariots, shields and helmets; in fact, most of them just had a single sword. 'Amateurs,' muttered the general under his breath.

He clicked his tongue, strode out of his tent, assembled his men and began to bark orders. Explaining the lie of the land, he rehearsed them into arrowhead formations, zigzags, points and wedges until they were like one compact war machine made up of interconnecting parts.

And while he watched them at their manoeuvres, he considered how the Britons were all spirit and no strategy. As unruly as leaves blowing in the wind, they were a collection of solo fighters and virtuosos, who dissipated themselves shouting, invoking the gods, beating clappers and singing random airs. But there were loads of them! He had only 15,000 soldiers whereas, if reports were correct, Boudicca had 200,000. The general raised his wrinkled brow to the horizon, wishing for more troops to arrive and fearing for his reputation in Rome. He paced and cracked his knuckles. No troops came.

Even as they approached the battle site, Boudicca knew her tightly woven war cloth was beginning to unravel; the strings of the loom were beginning to bend and snap. She couldn't keep a handle on the mass of warriors that were becoming out of control. Was she the only one that saw the whole war cloth? Her people devoted too much time taunting and torturing their victims and not enough time speaking to the gods of air and earth. There was too much drinking, too much boasting and now, with the prospect of victory, too much buffoonery around – imitating the blank expressions of their enemies, their mechanical marching, their excessive armour and mimicking their fat, mad Emperor Nero. Still she couldn't demand only incite. They saw her as Andraste and she had played up to it, leading by example, raising her arms to the moon and the sun, making the most of sudden flocks of birds and flashes of light, but now that the war threads were spinning off, fraying in every direction, who knew where it would end?

As the battle began, it was instantly clear to Boudicca that, unlike her, the Romans were leaving nothing to chance. First came the legionnaires, the front liners, each had a gladii, a short sword of around 30cm, and a smaller dagger; behind them came the infantry with their 3m javelins, followed by the cavalry on horseback with long lances. The Britons fell like corn, crushed by the threshing shields and swords of an army carefully orchestrated by Seutonius, marching ever forward, thrusting and slashing, using the dead as their pavement.

As Boudicca saw her people falling to the left and to the right, she found herself thinking of the hare that had promised them victory. It had run to the left, but who knew what twists and turns it took when it got to the forest? That was the trouble with divination – it never saw quite far enough. With her impeccable timing, she threw her tartan cloak round the shoulders of her daughters and they disappeared into the forest. From her belt she took a leather pouch containing a combination of hemlock, yew, bryony, buttercup, belladonna and thorn apple. She shook back her own rough hair, smoothed the soft curls of her daughter's and urged them to take the powder, rather than be at the mercy of their enemies.

'Live by your own rules and die by your own hand!' The poison threw them against the trees and on to the grass with such violence that they danced like maddened dryads in a grove.

The Romans had a final piece of luck. The families of the Britons who had come to watch the downfall of their hated invaders, had lined up their wagons behind their own soldiers and had been cracking nuts and suckling their babies, watching the show. As the bloodbath commenced, the warriors found themselves hemmed in by line upon line of wagons. There was no escape for fighters or audience. Boudicca's war cloth was trampled into the mud, soaked and reddened with blood. Nearly 80,000 Britons died in the final battle, compared to 400 Romans. The general hunted down any survivors and exacted such a terrible retribution that Rome hardly celebrated the victory, fearing it might stir up another revolt.

In a very short time, a bigger and better Londinium was rebuilt and Romanisation continued apace. The city they created covered roughly the same region as the City of London district today. If you walk through it now, you may happen upon a market, with fresh, brightly coloured fruit displayed on fake green grass. Maybe some of the market hawkers might catch your eye. Their timeless faces that have been folded into deep creases by the cold, early starts, snappy jokes and the constant packing and unpacking of their ripening and decaying produce, could have come from AD 70.

But despite the rebuilding, Boudicca's feisty spirit remains as much a part of London as that layer of burnt red earth. Some feel it strongest in the Kings Cross area, the part once known as Battle Bridges. It was there, so they say, that the Battle of Watling Street took place – the Britons' terrible defeat. Some even claim that the queen was buried under Kings Cross Station, platform 10. And you can see her ghost there now and again.

But to my mind, if you really want to sense her ancient presence, turn your back on the bustle, and your feet from the streets of the city. Walk north until you're deep in the peace of Epping Forest. Take a mossy path up through a line of giant beeches, until you reach Cobbins Brook. There, beyond the reach of motor cars and even mobile phones, is a great earthwork known by several different names: Castrum de Eppynghatthe or Ambresbury Banks or, locally, Boudicca's Last Stand.

4

LONDON BRIDGE

London Bridge is falling down,
Falling down, falling down.
London Bridge is falling down,
My fair lady.

It was the Romans who built the first London Bridge. They decided that the ford the Britons had used before would be wholly inadequate for the hordes of soldiers and civilians, chariots and carts, horses and donkeys, cattle, sheep, pigs, geese, and all manner of other beasts that they confidently and correctly anticipated would wish to pass over to their new city on the north side of the river. The Britons' old 'settlement' was barely worthy of the name, as far as they were concerned; just a poor cluster of huts and a wooden fortress. And it was only defended by a simple timber palisade. That was the first thing the Romans replaced, and in good solid stone, too. Proper city walls. They were built to last. And they did.

They did find one thing of interest. In the middle of the old encampment, there was a fine menhir, presumably a marker stone of some sort. It was not local stone. One very old man told them that his father remembered hearing that the stone had come from Troy long ago. Although that was clearly nonsense, the Romans left the menhir standing where it was, and decided they would use it as the central milestone for their new city, from which roads would lead in all directions. So they called it after their name for the city, the Stone of Londinium.

As for the bridge itself, that was built in wood, resting on a heavy bed of clay and small stones, which had to be built up very high into an embankment on the southern side because it was so marshy. They called that part the South work, which eventually became the name of the poor settlement that grew up there, on the south side of the bridge.

> Build it up with wood and clay,
> Wood and clay, wood and clay,
> Build it up with wood and clay,
> My fair lady.

But even the Romans, experts in construction, must surely have underestimated the power of the Thames' tides. Or perhaps they were relying on other ways to strengthen the bridge. 'Giving it a bit of spirit' you might call it. In time-honoured fashion that was done by choosing a living creature and burying it within the structure, thereby ensuring that its ghost or essence would always remain there to protect it. It might involve an animal, particularly a black dog, or sometimes a child, or sometimes a woman.

It was the latter, they say, who was selected to watch over London Bridge. My Fair Lady indeed, although how fair she was by the time she was through no one knew. Because the point was not to see her, but to be aware she was there, and perhaps, if you needed to, hear her. And though many scoff and say there is no proof, no evidence of the tale to be found in the foundations of the bridge, people have heard and sensed things that are equally hard to explain over the years.

A reputable man, a beadle of Borough Market, said a colleague had told him about a time when he was working nights there. Borough Market is right under the end of London Bridge, spreading into the street, and they used to patrol the whole area, up and down, all night long. They had to check everywhere then, though not anymore.

But anyway, that night this other beadle was by the steps up to the bridge. And all of a sudden he heard a girl scream. There is a little alleyway by the side of the church, inside the railings, and it was coming from there. Now he was the sort of man who had no sense of danger, and so he ran up and jumped over the railings and had a look. But he couldn't see anything. He went all round, but there was no one there. So he came back out and onto the pavement, and while he was walking down the street they call Winchester Walk, he heard it again. 'He told us, you know, there was nothing. But he heard it. They were laughing at him, the other lads – we all were – but it was serious. He meant it. It makes you think,' the beadle said to me. It did.

It has made people think each time they rebuilt the bridge as well. Which they had to do a lot because it was always falling down, just as the songs says.

> Wood and clay will wash away,
> Wash away, wash away,
> Wood and clay will wash away,
> My fair lady.
> London Bridge is falling down …

It must have been a nuisance for most Londoners. But what is bad news for some is usually good news for others; it's an ill wind that blows nobody any good.

In the time of King Edgar the Peaceful, the River Thames refused to take notice of the peace specified by his majesty. It swelled and swirled and rose so high from the gales and sea storms and moon-dragged tides that London Bridge was all but swept away. As it was, and continued to be right until the eighteenth century. Being the only permanent link with the other side of the city, people went to terrible trouble to try to cross the Thames by other means – and usually failed. Others tried to get across the remnants of the now very rickety bridge. And usually failed, too. Frequently fatally.

King Edgar himself had a flat-bottomed royal barge with at least six men to row it to and fro. He was extremely proud of it, but reluctant to lend it to anyone else. A few well-to-do nobles followed his example, and had barges built. But most individuals could not afford to pay six people to just row one across the river. However, one or two were very canny, and found a way of building something that was in between a boat and a barge, and was large and flat and fairly light, but heavy enough to be steady when several sat inside. And these could be rowed across the river by just one strong man – when the tides were right, of course. Sometimes with ropes tied to the other side for extra support. They called them ferries, and you'd pay a levy to be ferried across. So when times were bad for the bridge, they began to be good for the ferries and the ferrymen.

One such man was John Over, named after his trade, as everyone was in those days, for he carried passengers over the river to one side, and then back over again. Over and over all day long, and all week too and he started to make money, and from one ferry he'd now got two. And so it went on very nicely. Before long he had a team of ferrymen rowing for him. And a little house, then a bigger house, and then a grand house. On the north side, now. That was where everyone who was anyone lived. And now that he had made a fair bit of money, a fortune in fact, he felt that he was someone too. And it was time to forget about his roots, and Southwark, the place he'd come from, which was the poor side of the river, the poor side of town.

That might have been fine if he'd been on his own, but he wasn't. He had lost his wife, but he had a lovely daughter, and her name was Mary. And Mary had been happy in Southwark. Because she had her eye on a nice young man, and he'd had his eye on her. His name was Gerald, and his father was a cobbler, and he was learning to be a cobbler too; and even a shoemaker if he could be, for they are the ones who make, rather than merely mend. And Gerald set his sights high, and meant to do as well as he could.

But when you're rich, and getting richer, who wants a cobbler for a son-in-law? Even a good one would never be good enough for John Over. So poor Mary was told that her romance was over, and that she was to settle down on the north side of the river, and learn to be a lady. 'On no account,' said her father, 'are you to see that young man again. I will find a better match for you, never fear.'

But of course she did fear; in fact she dreaded the future, because she saw the sort of match he was lining up for her. And she saw what being rich was doing to her father. And she was wise enough to see that no good would come of either. For her father couldn't keep pace with himself. The more money John Over got, the more that he wanted. And the less he wanted to let go of it. He wanted it seen but not spent.

So he would eke out this, make Mary do without that, snitch and pinch from here and there, and the more he saved the more he minded any money going out. There was no doing without servants, or house slaves, not for a man of his station. But there was, he thought, no need for them to eat and drink so much. Enough to ruin him! He kept a close watch on the food supplies and a sharp eye on the cellar stores, and he became certain both were reducing at an alarming and rather suspicious rate. 'Surely,' he thought, 'there must be some way to cut consumption down?' And to cut out altogether the snacking and sipping and petty theft he suspected. But what on earth could he do? The problem worried and worried at him until he could not sleep and would barely eat, and he grew very thin. In the end Mary had to get a physician in. 'Because,' she told her father, in defence of the expense, 'I don't want you to die.'

And that's what gave John Over his brilliant idea: how to save enough money to pay for a physician twenty times over. For in those days, when somebody died, of course you'd have a wake, for one or two or even three days, and naturally, to show proper respect, the family and household would abstain from all indulgences. That meant, as far as possible, and in accordance with the wishes of the deceased, to a greater or lesser extent, that they would fast. John realised with delight that the whole household fasting to its greatest extent would save him a great deal of money. Especially if he specified his wake must last three days. And what was more, he began to think, if the servants thought he was dead and gone, and looking at his maker now, and not watching them at all, why then it would be the perfect chance for him to see exactly what they got up to secretly.

So when the physician arrived, John was very pleased to see him, for he had plenty to discuss with the good man, to the advantage of them both. So the two soon made a deal, and the physician put a grave face on, and said John was very ill. And next thing he was dying, and then the priest was rushing in for the last rites, and then the word was given out that he was dead.

Poor Mary. Before she had time to know what was what, they were having the wake. And she had loved her father, mean though he'd been. So she was weeping and wailing, and all in black, top to toe, even her hair, even her head, covered up entirely. And their mirror was too – even though it was special to own one of them, then, so you'd normally have them on show. But now it was John Over who was the centrepiece. He was lying in his coffin, laid out in state in the middle of the great hall, dressed in his best and looking rather grand, with candles around, and the onion in the coffin (in case the corpse got whiffy), decently hidden from view.

Now some people take wakes seriously, and some people think they need a bit of lightness and laughter too, just to help people get through them. But there was no respite at John Over's wake. It was a grave and a glum affair. Apart from Mary, it was mainly the household, plus a few of the ferrymen who'd worked for him. The notables of the town had been and gone, as swiftly as they could politely do. His friends had all been left behind in Southwark.

So everyone was sitting round, hoping someone else would speak. But no one knew quite what to say. To be honest, no one had been that fond of him. Except for his daughter, but then she had had no choice. And after all she'd been through – weeping and wailing, and before that watching over him, and worrying about him – well she was worn out, and she'd fallen asleep in a corner. So she wasn't saying anything either.

In all that silence, the only thing you could hear was the rumbling of stomachs. Only natural, really, they'd been fasting for a day and a night already. The ferrymen in particular were used to eating a big 'noon-meat', essential fuel if they were to pull their weight across the water. The slaves and the servants too had been up since dawn the day before, for they had had to fit the housework in as well. It didn't feel healthy to be going on empty. And once Mary's womanservant put her foot down, 'she must have a rest, poor thing, she's so done in', and made two strong ferrymen help carry Mary off to bed – well, there was no one there who might care the if the fast didn't last.

Anyway, not everyone thought thirst a required part, so now they all agreed that some small ale wouldn't count. So the serving woman went to the cellars for some pots, and the head man hurried after because now they were kept locked. As he was waiting with the keys, he noticed how much wine there was. A shame if it went to waste, for Mary never did touch much. Wouldn't it be the right thing done, if they all had a cup just to toast the old man? And after all, he thought, he won't miss it now he's gone. But upstairs and down with a jug was such trouble, he thought he'd be wise and bring up a barrel.

The mourners did mean to take just one cup of course. Only enough to drink the toast. But you know what wine does on an empty stomach. It goes straight to the head. So one drink led on to another, to another, and before they knew what they'd done, the whole of the barrel was gone. But then there was another one. And plenty more to come. Then everything was coming out, all restraint gone, the cook was bringing dishes up, the servants laying out the best, and everyone amongst them was having a fine feast. Except, of course, for John.

John Over, he was lying there, gritting his teeth. But they were all so merry drunk now, no one looked to see. And the party was still getting louder and louder, each person trying to outdo the other, until John's personal manservant capped the lot. 'There's still the best yet!' he cried, 'Look what I've got!' and he waved the only key to the master's treasure box.

John held his breath, for he guessed what was next. The man ran out, and soon came back carrying, very carefully, an almost priceless glass bottle of old French brandy. It was the most impressive gift John Over had ever been given. He'd kept it for years, for the ultimate occasion. And when he saw his servant with that bottle in his hand, it was far too much for John Over to stand. Up he leapt and over he ran to wrest his treasure back.

Well when that servant saw his master, who had so sadly died, suddenly and most unnaturally deciding to arise, he did what anyone would do if threatened by such an unexpected and alarming apparition. He defended himself with whatever he had to hand. Thwack! Down it came, and crack! It met its master's head. Sad to say, the bottle was broken, wasting all that was inside. And John Over's head was broken too, equally wasting all within. For that was the death of him.

So now the wake had to happen all over again. This time it had a proper corpse, although perhaps not looking quite as grand as it had done before. And this time there was no pretence of abstinence. Everyone needed a drink.

After the wake, John Over was duly buried, despite initial objections from the physician. And it was when that was over, that Mary realised she was very wealthy indeed – and alone. But there was no need to be lonely. For now she was both rich and free, she could marry who she pleased.

So she sat down at once, took out her quill and wrote to Gerald. That was one skill she'd gladly got from learning to be a lady. It had enabled them to stay in touch, while she still kept her father's command 'never to see him'.

'My love, please come, for I am free, if you still wish to marry me.'

Gerald wasn't quite as good at his letters as Mary was, but he had no difficulty in getting the gist of her message. He sent his reply back by return over London Bridge, which by now had been patched up so that people could pass, providing the weather was good enough.

'As soon as I finish my work tomorrow, I will be with you. My love is true,' came the reply.

Mary, you can be sure, went joyfully to bed that night. But then she was disturbed by the strangest of dreams. St Crispin, the patron saint of cobblers and shoemakers, came to her and whispered in her ear, 'Be sure and tell your love not to hurry too much. He must come to you only on his own shoes.'

Well, she woke up confused as to what the dream meant, but nevertheless, she sent Gerald another message, faithfully repeating what the saint had said. But the wind was blowing on the bridge that day, and the message was a bit delayed. And having got the first message, Gerald naturally wasn't waiting around for another. His kindly master, the shoemaker, even let him leave a little early, for everyone likes to see true love triumph. And Gerald had hired a horse, so he could travel in style. Head high, face wreathed in smiles, he rode out over London Bridge.

Maybe it was the bridge that shook, maybe it wasn't flat underfoot, but all of a sudden the horse cast a shoe, and stumbled. And poor Gerald was thrown right off, and broke his neck.

Poor Mary Over. Not much luck in that horseshoe, was there? Without her love, she lost all taste for London life. She sold the goods and house her father had left her, and with the money built a house for holy sisters, a little priory church in Southwark, which by and by was known as St Mary Overie; and years after was subsumed in Southwark Cathedral. It was right beside the south end of London Bridge, placed so close that all within might look up, if they wished, to make sure all who went that way were safe. There Mary retreated to pass her life in peace. And when she came to die, she was buried underneath, perhaps united now at last with her beloved Gerald.

Lost love and lost life. Was that their sacrifice? Was this Mary's offering of spirit strength to the new London Bridge? For it was thanks to her, and the profits of John Over's ferry business, that money was available for essential rebuilding work. London Bridge was much improved with wooden towers at each end, and it was made so wide, two oxen wagons could travel along it side by side. Most impressive of all, the great weight was held up by oaken piles, sunk into the river bed beneath the bridge and standing straight upright – like living oak trees, only that they were quite bare. No hopes there of roots and shoots and new green growth.

Build it up with seasoned oak,
Seasoned oak, seasoned oak,
Build it up with seasoned oak,
My fair lady.

But the bridge was barely restored before Edgar the Peaceful died and it wasn't long before the crown was in the unsteady hands of Æthelred the Unready, the 'Redeless one.' Then the Danes came again to harry England, led by their King, Sweyn Forkbeard. They sailed up the Thames with the tide, intending to raze London to the ground, and to burn the bridge down. But the citizens of

London, young and old, were so stoutly bold that they beat the Danes back.

And Æthelred followed unwise advice, as always, and paid for peace with bribes, £10,000 Danegeld fees, and then thrice that much again. Raised from taxes that all but broke the backs of the English, and Londoners most of all. But even worse, soon after, the king commanded the slaughter of all Danish settlers living in England. And in all of this, they say, the king was guided by the serpent tongue of Edric Streona, 'the refuse of mankind'.

Through this last disastrous decree, Æthelred murdered Sweyn Forkbeard's own sister, and brought upon them the full force of the Danish King's revenge. And this time, by blockades across the Thames, the Londoners were starved into submission. Then the Danish fleet sailed in, settling their ships along the river and their men in Southwark, and took charge of London Bridge, and so controlled the city. That might have been the end of Anglo-Saxon London then, and certainly the end for Æthelred, if he had not persuaded King Olaf of Norway to come onto his side.

King Olaf came with his Norsemen, and he saw how well the Danes could fight from London Bridge. They used it to attack, and to defend. They had towers on each side, and high barricades, to hide from spears thrown or arrows fired. But when his ships came below they could shoot and drop down stones, so no one could come close or pass beneath. And one more thing he took note of. The great oak piles on which the bridge depended.

Then Olaf knew that in order to win, they must take the bridge away from the Danes. But no one understood what he meant by that, except for his own Norse friends. Together they went down the river to where there were old houses built of wood and wattle and daub. These they took down, and bound them together to make strong shields of wood. Then they held them over their longships, as if they were great roofs.

Now they were ready to row upstream to the bridge. Their shields saved them from the Danish arrows and when they got near, from the worst of stones, and they rowed so fast that they just got through and under the bridge itself. There they were safe from the Danes' reach, and they waited for the tide to turn. Then they filled a small boat with rotten wood, and set fire to it against an oak pile, so the flames licked all the way up and at last the bridge began to smoke.

Seasoned oak will burn and smoke,
Burn and smoke, burn and smoke,
Seasoned oak will burn and smoke,
My fair lady.

In the confusion, Olaf and his men tied ropes and cables as low as they could around the great oak piles. Then, when the tide was going out, they rowed with the river, as hard as they might, towing these ropes behind. Now, the current of the River Thames and the pull of the men between them was so strong that the oak piles were dragged out of place at the base. Then London Bridge, with its great weight of men and heavy piles of stones, with creaks and groans and cries and moans, came tumbling down into the river. And with the bridge that day were drowned the men and hopes of Denmark.

But when it became known that King Olaf had pulled down London Bridge, he was hailed by the people of England, and Norway too, as a hero above all others. And his scalds made praise songs about him, which echo down to this day:

London Bridge is broken down.
Gold is won, and bright renown.
Arrows singing, Shields ringing,
Odin makes our Olaf win!

Later, Olaf was converted from the old religion to the new Christianity, and after he died, he was beatified. And that is how the people of London remembered him. A true saint. Now he is known as St Olave, as in St Olave's church and school. And in the root of Tooley Street, too.

It was not up to Olaf, of course, to rebuild London Bridge, which was done using wood again, for the interim. Nor did Olaf select the sacrifice to strengthen it. But, caught between Odin and early Norse Christianity as he was, he would probably have agreed with the bloody nature of the final choice …

For spilt blood was inevitable while Edric Streona was still around. And somehow, in true snake style, he managed to wriggle out of all blame for the trouble he had caused, and continued to pour his poison into the ears of kings, including the Danes, and Canute, son of Sweyn.

The only man who never listened to Streona was Edmund Ironside, the son of Æthelred, but as ready and as steady as anyone could be. Nicknamed on account of his legendary strength, he was a giant of a man, the Anglo-Saxons only true answer to the Danish invaders. Canute conquered much of England and was made king by the Witan parliament, but London rebelled and declared for Edmund, who was crowned king at Old St Paul's.

The battle between the two kings was an even match, but when Edmund challenged Canute to fight in single combat, and so reduce the bloodshed of their men, Canute refused for fear of facing such a mountain of muscle. Instead, he suggested dividing England in two, with Edmund keeping London, East Anglia, Wessex and Essex, and Canute having the rest. They agreed that this would stand until one of them died, when all lands would revert to the survivor.

This coalition was not easy for either ruler, particularly Canute, as London was so central to trade. One evening, Edric Streona, who had wormed his way into Canute's court, having double-crossed the Anglo-Saxons once too many times, happened to overhear Canute in one of his famous rages. 'That obdurate Edmund and his accursed London!' he stormed. 'Always in my way! If any man can move him I swear I'll raise them higher than any other ever was in England!'

Eager to squirm his way higher up the ladder, Edric took him at his word. Besides, he hated Edmund. Of course he was afraid to approach him openly, so he sent his sons to do the task. And it was done in such a dishonourable way, and in so private and disgusting a place, that no one would imagine it might happen. For the sons of Streona went to the privy, and positioned their crossbow in the midden heap, to fire up at Edmund as he sat upon the seat. It is said that the shaft went in so deep, that it could never be taken out again. And some say, because of that, it was not seen, and so not known at once as foul murder.

With Edmund dead, Canute became King of all England. He was a good ruler, level-headed and respected, even in London, although he made the citizens pay for having opposed him, by increasing the taxes on the city. When there, he occupied a fort by the Roman walls, where the River Fleet came to meet the Thames. Perhaps it was there that he famously taught his courtiers not to exaggerate his powers, by making them stand with him on the river beach, and commanding the Thames not to let the tide rise. He waited until it came almost to their waists before he allowed them all to escape. 'Now you have felt the power of such a thing,' he said, 'understand how weak beside it is the power of a king.'

At Christmas, Edric Streona, now restored to the Earldom of Mercia, was in London with the king. Ever wily, Edric had kept his knowledge about Edmund's death strictly secret, biding his time to speak to his best advantage. Late into the evening, he and King Canute were drinking and playing a game of chess. Edric rather unwisely won, and then even more ill-advisedly argued with the king about the rules. Canute flew into a terrible temper, and Edric, anxious to turn the tide back in his favour, played what he thought was his trump card. He told the king all about the murder of Edmund, and, smiling, explained he had done it at Canute's request. He even reminded him of what he had sworn, to 'raise the man who removed Edmund higher than any other'.

Canute was absolutely horrified. Earl Edric was drawn by the heels from the fort, scorched by flaming torches and then had his head struck off. His body was thrown down into the ditch, where the hungry hounds prowled, just outside the city walls. It is remembered to this day by the name of Houndsditch. But they say even dogs didn't want to eat that meat.

Yet the king still kept to the letter of his oath. Edric Streona's head was stuck on a long spike, and hoisted high above London Bridge – higher than any other man had ever reached.

And Edric's blood dripping down below provided a human offering to be absorbed by Canute's newly rebuilt London Bridge.

It started a tradition, too, for putting traitor's heads up there, which was to be continued for centuries, conveniently answering the needs of many a reincarnation of the bridge – including what was presumed to be the final one, King John's utterly indestructible structure of stone.

> Build it up with solid stone
> Solid stone, solid stone,
> Build it up with solid stone,
> My fair lady.

Almost invincible – depending on the weather. But that never is dependable in London. As the old riddle says: 'As I went o'er London Bridge I heard a great crack. Can any man in England ever mend that?' No man could, for the problem – which recurred many times – was ice. Packed around the stone it was cold enough to crack it, as they saw before too long when the Thames froze solid.

> Solid stone, will crack and fall,
> Crack and fall, crack and fall,
> Solid stone, will crack and fall,
> My fair lady.

But fortunately not only did successive royal dynasties supply sufficient human heads, but also, along with many London citizens, they were wealthy and wise enough to realise the economic necessity to rebuild the bridge every time it cracked and fell. Although, it must have seemed like it was literally made of money!

> Build it up with silver and gold,
> Silver and gold, silver and gold,
> Build it up with silver and gold,
> My fair lady.
> Thieves will steal it away,
> Steal away, steal away …

Set a watch all night and day,
Night and day, night and day…
What if he should fall asleep?
Fall asleep, fall asleep …

Set a pipe between his teeth,
'Twixt his teeth, 'twixt his teeth,
Set a pipe between his teeth,
My fair lady.

So by all these diverse means, Londoners ensured that their bridge continued structurally and spiritually strong and safe until the eighteenth century, when a brother bridge was constructed to share the traffic, and the old one shored up in a new way. Better than ever:

Build it up with bricks and mortar,
Bricks and mortar, bricks and mortar,
Build it up with bricks and mortar,
My fair lady.

Bricks and mortar will not stay,
Will not stay, will not stay …

Build it up with iron and steel,
Iron and steel, iron and steel,
Build it up with iron and steel,
My fair lady.

Even in the most modern times, with a huge range of building material available, London Bridge still had to be rebuilt from time to time. And that of course posed a whole new problem. For Queen Elizabeth II the possibility of immuring someone inside London Bridge when it had to be replaced in 1973 was simply not an option. Nor was the chop-chop at the block and then hang the head up solution available to her, as it had been to her namesake, Elizabeth I.

After much head scratching, a clever alternative was suggested. The Fair Lady should be the Queen herself. What better head than hers? Not removed from her in the flesh, as has happened to queens in the past, but simply represented as she is in every hand in every purse, in every grubby transaction and great commercial enterprise. Heads or tails, the coin spins. And that was what was used. A sovereign to represent our sovereign, head facing up, implanted in the bridge.

In the twenty-first century too, London Bridge has, to some extent, been renewed. Only a few years ago I was walking along it, picking my way through extensive roadworks; men with big machines, and steaming tarmac cooling to a flat black path. One of the first to walk across it, I remembered the old tradition, wondering if anyone thought of it now. And suddenly I saw something shining. It was only a penny but a gleaming new one. Not just dropped but pressed in deep, to lie properly flush – Queen's head up.

5

WILLIAM I AND SONS

For a king to ensure his succession, in the days when daughters were disregarded, he had to have a son. At least one, but preferably two, because you never knew … Chances of survival weren't that good. But any more and you may be sure that as well as options, you would have opposing forces, which would probably disrupt the direct line anyway.

William the Bastard of Normandy was well aware of that. After all, his claim to the English throne was extremely indirect. A circuitous family connection, and a promise made by Edward the Confessor that was afterwards denied. Besides that, he had to fight Harold Godwinson, who had been declared king with most of England's thegns or landed lords supporting him.

But perhaps William was right to claim that he had been divinely ordained to reign. And Harold should have understood that the message he'd seen in the heavens was not, after all, so good. For the 'star with a fiery tail', Halley's Comet, had appeared that year, just after Edward, dying, declared Harold as heir.

Or maybe it was simply good tactical timing. Godwinson had barely beaten the Viking Hardrada in the north before he was forced to march to meet with William of Normandy in the south. For whatever reason, it was the Saxon cry of 'Goddemite' that was overcome by 'Dex Aie' – 'God Aid Us' – the Norman battle cry, at Hastings. King Harold died with an arrow in his eye, and his body was buried without a sign, so that no one might know where to go to honour him, or to cry for him.

Then the Dowager Queen gave up the Keys of England and William the Conqueror marched up to London town. The city gates were closed against him, and London Bridge was barred, but he bartered with the citizens, and bargains were soon struck. All London's privilege and rights would be retained, and most Saxon common laws remained.

William was welcomed into London then, and with impeccable timing once again, was crowned almost straight away. It was at Westminster, King Edward's newly built Abbey, on Christmas day, 1066. 'Unto us a king … '

At first King William I went easy on the reins. He hoped that not too much would have to be changed. It all depended on making alliances and friends amongst important London citizens and Saxon landed thegns.

But having Norman overlords affected almost everything. The Norman court, the way they thought, the language they talked, even the way they looked was different from the Anglo-Saxon, Danish, and Celtic mix that the English had become. William and his French friends seemed effete in many ways, their faces like beardless boys, for the Norman fashion was to be close shorn. Londoners guffawed when William struck a new coin, marked with his name 'Le Rei Wilam', and shamelessly put on his face, bare as a babe.

Under the Norman eye, women's clothing, and social position became less loose, a little more constrained; a closer fit that emphasised their female shape and feminine spirit. Several Saxon ladies, including wives of Harold's knights, were obliged to take up needles and stitch the Norman tale of victory at Hastings. The story was embroidered, enhancing the Conqueror's glory, so his chronicle became the new sung song, the history that was passed on.

But still red-headed William dared not sleep deep in his royal bed. Whenever he relaxed, and turned his back to keep an eye on Normandy or another of his territories, rebellions broke out in England, led by English men on whom he'd thought he could depend. He couldn't replace everyone with trusted Norman friends.

London above all made him uneasy. It was such a complex mix of races, rules and rights, especially 'freemen' of the city who paid

taxes to the king. Even an apprentice could hope to become one of them, yet these were the powerful citizens who had made William king – and possibly might try one day to 'unmake' him again.

They were too independent, with all their rights to trade, and parade, and vote at the Folkmoot. Unruly too – he knew they were plotting and planning all around in that ugly English consonant harsh tongue, so unpleasant to hear, and impossible to understand. Uncivilised lot, he thought; didn't even eat properly with a fork. Just a knife for everything, and the blades were as sharp as could be; altogether too knife happy as far as he could see.

So William decided he must show his strength, and do something to put Londoners in their place. He had a tower built by the river, into the Roman wall, on the site where the Romans had a bastion centuries before. It was on the little hill beneath which Bran's head lay. He commissioned a Norman style motte and bailey, but square rather than round, and much bigger than normal, made of solid stone. It was clearly a good treasury, and a formidable defence, but above all this new 'Tower of London' was intended to impress. And oppress as well, for Londoners saw it was built to control, not to protect them all.

The Conqueror, however, was content. For the present, at least, the problem was solved. But being a restless man, he soon began looking ahead, and envisaging difficulties to come. For what would happen to his lands when he was gone? He had amassed a huge amount and he wanted it all to be kept, and looked after and accounted for, so it could be used to best effect. He had sent his men all over the country, collecting information. Every town and village and household was neatly noted down. Who belonged to what, and what exactly they had got, and most important, how much tax was due. Every wood, common, hill and hollow, every farm and field, fertile or fallow. All accounts were bound together, into the great Domesday Book.

William knew exactly what he had at his disposal. And he didn't want it squandered and lost the moment he shut his eyes and died. But keeping it all in one pair of hands required a certain sort of man, like himself, with an eye on everything. He did not expect that ability in any of his sons; only that they would fight for succession as soon as he was gone. No. It would be better to divide his lands between them. But who should get what? Unable to decide, he asked his councillors.

The king's advisers were wise indeed, or they would never have survived at court, which was a place of whispers and intrigue. Consequently, they did not offer their opinions directly.

'Majesté,' they said, 'the natures of your kingdoms are so different. And the same is true of your young sons. Look into their hearts, and you will see who suits which part.'

'And how may I do that?' demanded William.

'Tell them to go to your Tower of London, and let us talk to them there, one by one. And you, Majesté, should listen privately.'

So when the time came, the king and his councillors climbed to the top of the tower and the king hid himself behind a door, where he could hear all, but could not be seen.

Robert, his eldest son, tall and finely dressed, was first to come up the steps. From that height they could see for miles in all directions.

'Young Sire,' said one councillor. 'Please can you tell me, if God had made you as a bird, which one might you wish to be?'

Robert looked around him slowly, and then paused, eyes on the east and the wild open marshes. 'I would be a goshawk,' he said. 'It is the noblest of all birds.'

'What signifies the choice my first son made?' the king asked afterwards.

'The goshawk's name is *gentilus* which means nobility indeed,' the councillors explained. 'Your son is a knight at heart, a brave fighter, independent, yet obedient to a master. But hawks fly far from home, forgetting all in the chase.'

The next to come was William Rufus, red haired as his father. 'What do you want with me?' he asked. Again they asked him to select a bird. William looked straight upwards, almost into the sun itself. 'I would be an eagle,' he said at once. 'It dominates all others.'

This time when the king asked, his men were slow to answer him. 'The eagle is a royal bird, but it lives by rapine. This son would be a king, but rule through fear, and never seek to know his people.'

The last son to come was Henry, the youngest and least regarded. They asked him the same question, and he thought for a long while, looking down towards the city, and smiling at the scene spread beneath him. The fields beyond the settlement still held within the walls, the bustling cheap, and the busy streets with shops and traders of all sorts, and nestling in between them the old church of All Hallows. Even high up as they were, they could hear and smell the force of the life bubbling below.

'I would be a starling,' he said with quiet certainty. 'It is a social bird, bright and debonair. It does not rob its neighbours and it has an excellent ear.'

'The starling is a common bird,' cried William when his son had gone. 'Of what use is one who prefers that?'

His advisers smiled. 'This prince would be a man of peace, unless he had to fight,' they said. 'The starling, Pliny says, listens best and quickly learns all tongues; he has heard one speak in Latin and in Greek. So, hearing all men, your son would learn how to govern them.'

William remembered the wisdom of his councillors, and on his deathbed he divided up his lands and goods accordingly. England he bequeathed to cruel William Rufus, so this rough land might be subdued by an iron hand. Normandy, more civilised, he left to Robert, the noble knight. To Henry, he gave silver and his personal treasures, to enable him to pursue the peaceful life of a learned man.

But perhaps the king's advisors were wiser in their forecasts than their master realised.

William Rufus, King of England, like an arrogant eagle, despising all beneath, disregarded the power of small birds to unite and find other ways to fight a predator. Hated by all for his ruthless rule, he was killed by an 'accidental arrow' when out hunting in the New Forest.

Robert, eager as any goshawk to fly high and fight, joined the First Crusade for glory and rich pickings. He paid twofold for his time away. It cost him his Norman lands, mortgaged to Henry to support the cause. And it lost him the moment to grab the English crown. Too late, he challenged his youngest brother. Beaten back like an aging hawk, he was then 'hooded' – held impotent, a captive in his father's tower.

Wealthy Henry 'Beauclerc' listened, and learned how to talk and connect with all. A social networker, he drew support together to help him claim the crown when Rufus died, and later to defeat his brother Robert. So the simple starling turned out to be the best bird of them all. And the sole successor of the Conqueror.

6

RAHERE

What chance of success is there in London if you are one of the poor? In medieval Norman times there was little to hope for unless you knew how to entertain. That's one way out that has never changed. Especially if you can make people laugh. Rahere could do that easily enough. He was a natural mimic, with an ever-ready wit, and an excellent ear for everything. He could sing any song, even if he'd only heard it once, and play any instrument that had strings. But most of all, he had such *joie de vivre* himself that he couldn't help transmitting it to everybody else.

Not that you would have thought he had much to be merry about. He came from a poor family, with many children too. From the first he longed to be noticed, but what was he to do? It was the hardest of harsh times then – the Red King William Rufus' reign. No opening for anyone except the King's few friends.

But it seemed Rahere was born under a lucky star after all. For it wasn't long before the hated red-headed king died. It was most unexpected – an accident with an arrow. Fortunately, his brother Henry was there to pick up the reins of power.

Of course nothing changed overnight, and some barely even noticed the difference. But little by little English life began to improve for many. Opportunities opened, and the effects trickled down.

For a start, Henry was the first Norman ruler to learn the English language. And he insisted it was spoken alongside French, even at the Norman court. Perhaps that was also because his wife, Matilda, was a Scottish princess of Anglo-Saxon stock. But the message was clear; the new King and Queen represented what England was to be – an Anglo-Norman alliance.

Soon there were jobs for all sorts at court. The great hall of Westminster palace, built by William Rufus, and one of the few things that he could be proud of, now buzzed with all manner of activities. Law-making, administrative reform and matters of state; clerics and learned men gathering for scholarly debate; writers and poets vying for *le mot juste* or cleverest rhyme; musicians blowing, plucking, strumming, drumming out time; feasting, drinking, singing, dancing, juggling and entertaining, romancing and love making. Affairs of every imaginable kind. Henry loved his queen but he had a big appetite and a taste for many a pretty face. And he set the pace. His court was notoriously gay. Infamously so, some might say. But what happens behind closed doors, especially in royal palaces, is probably best left ignored. Unless you want to play too.

Meanwhile Rahere was growing up fast. He discovered early on that food and sometimes money might be won if you could amuse someone. It had started quite simply in the street. He had just been playing, entertaining his brothers, and some soldiers passing by had stopped and watched. As they went on, one threw down a coin. It was a quarter of a round esterlin or penny. Rahere couldn't believe his eyes. Nor could his mother who happened to be watching, and had it off him before he even had time to admire the way it glittered in the sunshine.

After that, his family agreed, it would be a sin for him to waste such God-given skills. As he was lithe and light on his feet, and his fingers were nimble and quick, it didn't take him long to learn a range of clever tricks: juggling and jumping, wheeling and tumbling, balancing on one hand or two, or even on his head.

Soon he was ready to be sent out, sometimes with his brothers but mostly on his own, because that way he was more likely to want to hurry home after. It was frightening to be small and out late on your own. Not so much for fear of people, but more because of the animals, especially the pigs that'd be out in the street for any rubbish they could eat. A sow could give a nasty bite if you surprised her in the night.

As the years went by, Rahere got used to his work. He focussed on places where something was already going on, a Saint's-day parade, a wedding celebration, or maybe an execution. He was good at picking the right moment to begin – juggling perhaps, or playing the flute. When a crowd started to gather, he would play the fool, picking something up with his toes and trying to put it on his head, or pulling impossibly long ribbons from his nose. Once everybody was properly paying attention to him, he would sing. Something simple at first – a rhyme or verse maybe, making fun of someone standing round. Nothing nasty, just enough to make everybody else laugh. Then, if he thought it was worth going on, he would sing a proper song. And his voice that had seemed so ordinary would suddenly soar like an angel. He had the face to go with it too. Especially if it was reasonably clean.

His family were satisfied with what he got. But he himself was not. He began to long for something better altogether. Going around London as he did, wandering further and further afield, he saw so many different places, different kinds of people, different ways of living. He dreamt of life far beyond the realm of all possibility for a boy such as him. But he couldn't resist looking at it, at least. It was a long way to walk – the opposite end of town from his home – but that was for all the right reasons. It was because it was rich. It was where the nobility lived. The Thorney Island area.

Whenever he could, Rahere would go there, just to stand in the shadows and gaze at Westminster, pretending to himself that he, too, was part of the great palace. Sometimes, especially on feast days, you could see lords and ladies moving about, or even coming out, and then the crowds pressed as close as they dared to stare at their finery and rich attire. Rahere would watch the spectators too, and wonder how it felt to be so much admired.

But best of all he liked to stay out late at night, and cross over London Bridge to walk along the other side. Then in the distance he could see the Kings Hall of Westminster, light pouring from its great windows, reflecting on the river. Sometimes he'd even imagine he heard music coming from it. It seemed to him like heaven itself.

His ambition grew until, when he turned fourteen, he decided he would have to do something about it. Nothing ventured, nothing gained. He planned for weeks, perfected new tricks, and washed in the river every day to get his whole body as clean as he could.

He chose his time with care. Just after Easter. The king himself was at Westminster to enjoy a spectacle of some sort. Whatever it was, it had attracted the finest young men of his court. As they spilled out afterwards, Rahere was ready. Just by the bridge over the stream that he knew they would have to cross.

The light was beginning to go, so he was juggling with burning sticks. Attendants hurried up to clear him out of the way, but he dodged past, and turned it into a dance, tumbling and whirling, still holding the sticks, so the flames trailed after him. The pattern of light he made was dazzling. And at the same moment he started to sing. It was a song in French, calculated to catch the courtiers' attention. Sweet and yet soulful. And it suited his voice. Now several had stopped to watch. It was time to draw them in – perhaps to borrow something. That worked well if it was the right thing. And the right person too. He already knew what object to choose. But which of the men should it be?

He looked around and his eyes met those of a nobleman not much older than him. Twenty or so. Rahere bowed low, arms out to either side, and in the same movement he pushed his flaming brands into the ground so they lit all around. As he straightened up, his gaze found that same man, and their eyes locked.

Calmly, as if it was an everyday request, Rahere made it known that he would like to borrow the young lord's sword. 'If you please,' he added, in his best Norman French. He knew very few words, but his accent was excellent.

A ripple of uncertainty ran through the group. To hand over your weapon was a foolish thing to do, but the boy confused them – he seemed so much at ease and he sounded like a Norman too. And now he was mimicking them, showing them each so manly and tall, and then portraying himself as very small; it was absurd to think he could be a threat to them all. He did it so delightfully too. The nobleman relaxed and laughing tossed the boy his sword.

Rahere caught it by the hilt, as if well used to handling it, then pressed its point into the earth, and, leaning on it, levered himself up.

For a moment he hung balanced there, hand on sword, upside down, feet high up in the air. And then, unbelievably, he started to spin. How it was done I do not know; it was something new he had taught himself to do, and there is a picture of him doing it, in the church of St Bartholomew the Great. But that is running ahead of the tale.

For that moment back then changed everything. By the time Rahere had somersaulted back to his feet and solid ground, there were whistles and calls and cheers of applause from everyone around. With a flourish he pulled the sword free, wiped its point perfectly clean, and returned it to its owner. As he did, he looked him full in the face again, and then, very slowly, smiled. Rahere was good looking, but his smile was utterly beautiful. It lit him up from within; transformed him. He saw the reaction in the young man's eyes and turned as if to walk away.

'Wait!' the young lord cried. 'Walk with me a while.' And as they fell into step, he reached out his hand. 'Come young friend,' he said, 'when did you last eat?'

And so, Rahere walked into another kind of life. The pinnacle, he thought, of all his dreams. But he was destined to go higher still. For while he stayed with his new friend, Rahere learnt swiftly, watching and listening and seeing how he should behave to please all those around him. And so well did he do, it was soon hard to recognise the poor boy he had been. The nobleman was proud of his young protégé. When he thought that Rahere was ready, he took him to the royal court, and introduced him to the king.

That was how Rahere became King Henry's jester. And since he persisted in mastering every new instrument that came his way, it wasn't long before he was one of the king's favourite minstrels too.

He was surprisingly popular throughout the whole of the court. His cheerful wit was well appreciated in a place that set such store on skill with words. But he was careful to keep his jokes kind, though clever, for he could see that sharper tongues were apt to end up cutting themselves deepest. Rivalry was rife amongst the courtiers, and those most loved so often seemed to overreach themselves, and fall from favour, helped on their way down by many waiting restlessly below. Rahere steered a steady course, friendly to one and all, balancing between factions as skilfully as he had had to do upon the hilt of that first sword. And he was lucky, too, in finding influential support from a most unexpected source.

Queen Matilda was a deeply pious woman. Although she truly loved her husband, she was not fond of some of the pleasures of his court. Yet young Rahere she took under her wing. She liked his gentle playful nature, and she loved to hear him sing. And so she had him instructed in the music dearest to her heart – that of the Church. To help in this she also made sure that he was taught to read and write. Latin at first, of course, but when she saw his overwhelming thirst for knowledge, she encouraged him to study other languages as well. For Rahere, with his hungry mind, the ability to decipher script was a gift beyond all others; it opened the doors to people's thoughts, in lands he'd never dreamt of. And he repaid the queen with such devotion that she trusted him absolutely, and when her son Prince William was born, she thought there was no better playfellow to sing her child to sleep, and watch over his first steps, than young Rahere.

And so Prince William Adelin, the apple of King Henry's eye, and sole heir and hope of all of England, grew up treating Rahere as if he was an elder brother who could somehow always find the time to play or sing or tell him stories.

For Rahere that was the happiest of times. But destiny, it seemed, had other plans. When the prince was fifteen, Queen Matilda died. London went into mourning. The king was distraught. William sat in his in his mother's rooms and wished that he could weep in peace. But since such behaviour was not proper for a prince, he returned to court society, and tried to drown his grief in wild excess. And although he married the following year, and was instated as Duke of Normandy soon after that, his right royal indulgences went on unchecked. Even when Rahere reasoned with him, he failed to talk him into better sense.

That autumn, King Henry was returning with the prince from a visit with the King of France. It was after the harvest, they were laden with gifts, and fine French wine, of course. At the port, they met FitzStephen, a long-term friend of the family. It had been his father who had captained the ship that took the Conqueror to

England in 1066. Now FitzStephen was waiting with a ship of his own, built to be the swiftest in the fleet, according to a special new design.

'My White Ship is made to fly across the waves,' he boasted. 'We will carry you to Hastings, as my father took yours, but yet we will arrive in half the time!'

The king was sorry, he'd arranged to go with someone else, and they were due to sail within the hour. But Prince William was delighted to accept, and as the vessel was so fast he saw no need to hurry off. Besides, there was too much fresh wine to taste.

Long after the king had left, William and his entourage were dancing all along the shore and toasting the White Ship's success. They were enjoying themselves so much that they refused even to pause and let the priest come past and bless the new ship's boards.

By the time they set off it was dark, and most of the crew were also drunk. The lights of the king's ship, far ahead, had long since vanished out of sight. 'He could be landing before long,' a sailor said.

The prince's party took this as an affront. Determined not to arrive last, they challenged FitzStephen to make good his boast. 'Prove your ship is truly fast!' 'Overtake the king!' they cried.

And so the captain tried. He altered the course to make it more direct, though he might have guessed that in the night this was suicide. Not far from Barfleur port, they struck a submerged rock, and the ship very quickly capsized. A butcher survived because the ram skins he wore kept him warm and afloat until he was found at dawn. But everyone else was drowned.

William Adelin had been put into a boat, but climbed back to try to get his sister out. FitzStephen managed to swim up to the surface, but when he heard the prince was lost, he let himself go down.

It is said King Henry never smiled again. The flower of the royal youth gone in one swoop: two much-loved illegitimate sons, a daughter, a niece, dear friends, half of the English court and any hope of smooth succession to the throne all sank with William Adelin, heir to the English throne.

But while the country reeled with the tragedy, there were many who pointed the accusing finger. 'A judgement from God' they wrote, 'A punishment for the sins of the flesh.'

Rahere was overwhelmed with sorrow and a sense of guilt. He begged permission from the king to make a pilgrimage to Rome, to visit the shrine of St Paul, the patron saint of London, and to pray on behalf of them all. Henry readily agreed, and Rahere set out at once. Dressed as a penitent, in rough cloth, armed only with a pilgrim's staff, it was the first time for many years that he had felt the London streets beneath his bare feet. It was hard to have so little again, but yet he felt curiously free. Although, with only a small scrip of money, he soon remembered that there was no romance about being hungry.

Travelling by foot it was a journey of many months to Rome, and one that plenty did not survive. He must have thought of William Adelin as he lurched across the Channel, crammed in the ship's hold, with 100 other stinking and vomiting penny-paying passengers. It was a long walk down through France and a steep climb over the high snow-capped mountains into Italy. Rough too, sleeping in monasteries and pilgrim dormitories, sharing beds with others, fleas and lice. And in such close confines, diseases of all sorts passed from one to another as easily as greetings.

Rahere, however, did not get truly sick until he had arrived in Rome, and done penance for his sins to St Paul. As he had promised Henry, he visited the very spot where the saint was martyred – the Three Fountains – outside the city walls. This place was also famous locally, for mosquitoes. They carried a disease known as 'Roman fever', which nowadays we call malaria.

Rahere stayed there praying for several nights and soon found himself shivering and burning by turns, aching in every limb. Other pilgrims found him, and, seeing he was desperately ill, they carried him to the hospice of St Bartholomew. Although the monks there cared for him as best they could, everyone assumed that he would die.

But in his wild delirium, Rahere had a vision. It began with the roar of a thunderstorm which turned into a dreadful dragon-winged beast. Catching him up in its great clawed feet it carried him high, high, high into the air, then suddenly dropped him like an eagle might toss scraps to its young. He landed on a narrow ledge, and peering over the edge he saw an awful abyss. But far, far below he sensed something moving. Though terrified of falling, he felt an awful urge to see what it was.

Then, all at once he felt someone holding him safe, and it made him feel so calm, he was able to look deep down. Right at the bottom were many minute creatures, like insects swarming. But now he saw they were children playing, boys as ragged as he himself had been. And the place they were in was where he had grown up, Smithfield, in London. Where the smiths worked beside the horse pond and the Kings Fair was held every year. The ground was so boggy that it was never wholly dry, and in winter time it froze so hard that if you could find two sheep bones and strap them to your feet with strips of skin, then you could slide across the ice with tremendous speed. Rahere remembered the thrill of it even now. But as he looked he saw things he had never noticed then.

All around there were people in such poverty that their skin was hanging off their bones. Some had broken limbs, or hands that were missing fingers or thumb, or sores festering on faces and arms. It broke his heart to see it, and to think of the comfort he had lived in at the court. And there and then, he swore that if ever he should recover and return home to London, he would build a hospice for the poor where there was none; a place they could go for help and for healing, whether they could pay for it or not.

At that moment, once again, Rahere felt strong hands supporting him. And now he pulled back from the edge, and looked to see who it was. It was a man with a face of extraordinary sweetness and light in his eyes almost too bright to bear. 'I am Christ's apostle, St Bartholomew,' he said. 'I have come to help you, and to command you too. In that place that you have seen in your dream, you must build a great church in my name, and your hospice by its side. If you do what I ask, never fear; I will be here to support you in the task.'

Then Rahere felt his head clear, and his fever go. He opened his eyes and looked up. By his bed a priest was standing, ready to administer the last rites. Filled by the strength of his dream, Rahere returned directly to England and the king. And when Henry saw how changed he was, and how inspired, he promised him all that he required by way of land and money and authority too.

The land Rahere chose was the marshy flat expanse of Smithfield. And as soon as the building work began, three holy travellers came from the Byzantine Empire, as well as Alfune, one the wisest men of Christendom; they planned it together so it became a place where all could meet in brotherhood, and peace. The church was built with a priory on the south side, and a hospice for the poor beside it, and Rahere named it all St Bartholomew's. Even the Kings Fair that continued there every year was then called after the saint.

Rahere himself was the first prior, and he also presided over much of the healing that took place in the hospice. And even after his death, they say, the sick were healed, the blind could see, and the lame were made to walk again. Today you can still feel the strength of his spirit in the church. Some claim they have seen his ghost, too, by the altar. As for his hospice, it was moved and rebuilt elsewhere as St Bartholomew's Hospital. But even in this altogether different modern world, it remains a place that anyone in need of healing can go to, without having to pay.

7

WITCH WELL

Ding Dong Bell, Pussy's in the Well
What she does there
No one can tell.

Once upon a time, when pigs spoke rhyme, and London was a small place in anybody's mind, there were wells all around the town. Shepherds Well to Streatham Wells, Sadler's Well to St Chad's Well, Woodford Wells to Bagnigge Wells, St Bride's or Bridget's Well, Mossy Well or Muswell, Clerks Well to Camberwell, Briton's Well or Cripplewell. Some had fresh water, good for drinking, and there were always queues of children, women and water-carriers. Some had sweet water, good for healing, and people came to cure their sore eyes and stiff legs and sad hearts. Others again had scummy water that was good for hiding, and people came with all sorts of dark secrets, and threw bodies, bones, and even babies down there.

Now, in that long ago time when wells were all round and witches were as commonplace as apples, there was a man whose wife died, leaving him with a little girl. She was bright and willing but he couldn't manage on his own, so he married again before too long. His new wife had a daughter too, much of an age as his own, so that would be company for the child, he thought, as well as a mother to care for her.

But sadly it was the worst sort of company and no caring at all, for the new wife hated her stepdaughter from the moment she first clapped eyes on her, because her own child seemed as heavy and slow as a toad beside her. And mother and daughter between them made sure that young girl had such a hard time of it, it was a wonder she didn't run off altogether. But she was always hoping that somehow she might please them, and befriend them, and so she kept on trying. They made her work so hard, she was almost spinning in her sleep, seeing to the fires, cleaning the floors, cooking the food, mending and making all the clothes. She never had a moment to sit still.

Even when she went to get water from the well, and was waiting for the bucket to drop down to the bottom, she had to take out her spindle and spin. But that was a pleasure too, for her, because that little wooden spindle was one thing she still had left from her dead mother.

Then one day she was at the well, spinning while she peered into the dark depths to see if the bucket was full, and, 'oh dear!' the spindle slipped out of her hand, and fell down into the water. The poor girl was beside herself. She could not go back without her spindle, and so she jumped into the well after it.

To her surprise she found that, instead of landing in water, there was soft green grass beneath her feet. She looked about, and saw she was in another world altogether. There were fields all around her, with a little path running through. But right beside her was a well just like the one above, and on the little wall around it sat her spindle, safe and sound. So she slipped it into her apron pocket, and set off on her way.

She walked and walked and walked, but saw no one. Not even a bird or a bee. Then suddenly she heard a strange voice crying, 'I burn! I burn! I burn!'

She still couldn't see anyone, but just ahead there was an oven, all on its own, with a little wisp of smoke coming out. Hurriedly she opened the door, and inside was a loaf of bread, just beginning to burn at the edges. So she took it out as quick as could be, and laid it on the grass to cool.

'Oh, thank you, thank you,' said the oven. 'I hope one day I can help you too. Break off a bite of bread if you like.' Well she was very hungry, so she took a piece to eat, and went on her way wondering.

By and by, she heard a miserable moaning, 'I burst! I burst! I burst!' Before long she came to a cow, dripping milk, udders so full they were scraping the ground.

There was a bucket nearby, and milking stool too, so the girl sat down and set to. In no time the bucket was filled to the brim, and the cow was much relieved. 'Oh, thank you, thank you,' she mooed. 'I hope one day I can help you too. Drink as much as you like.' Well the girl was very thirsty, so she drank her fill, and went on her way wondering even more.

After a while she heard a creaking voice calling, 'I break, I break, I break!'

Around the corner there was an apple tree, its branches so loaded with big ripe fruit it was bent right to the ground. 'Pick me please,' said the apple tree. So she picked the apples into neat heaps until the tree could straighten up again.

'Thank you, thank you,' it rustled. 'I hope one day I can help you too. Take as many as you like.'

Well she did like apples, so she walked on munching, wondering more than ever.

At last she came to a dark wood with branches and brambles tangled all around the path. She pushed on through, and finally found a broken old gate to an empty garden, with a tumbledown house in the middle.

She knocked on the door and it opened with a screech, and there was an old witch, with a nose down to her knees, fingernails as long as knives, and eyes even sharper.

'Well,' she said, 'I suppose you want to eat and sleep, but it's nothing for nothing in this house. You're going to have to work for it, and hard too, or it will be the worse for you.'

'I can work hard,' said the girl, 'for a little wage and a place to stay.'

'Then you'd better come in,' said the witch with a grin, 'but watch the cat. She'll bite and scratch.'

The girl stepped back as a cat slid by, all teeth and claws and wild eyes.

'Now start,' said the witch. 'Straight away. Mend the gate, dig the garden, clean the house from top to bottom, fetch the water and the wood, and then you can cook my food. But there's one thing you must remember. Never, ever, ever look up the chimney. If you do I'll break your bones and bury you under the marble stones.'

So the girl got going, and when she was done, she was so worn out that she could barely see her own bite of food. But she didn't forget to save some for the cat, though she got little thanks from the beast for that.

And it went on like this, day after day, and if it didn't get any better, well it least it never got worse. But as for her wages, they never seemed to come, and when she asked the witch for them, all she got was a laugh.

Then one day the witch was out, and the cat was in, and prowling about. And all of a sudden it stopped, and stared at the girl, hard. 'You know what to do, don't you?' it asked.

'Goodness gracious!' said the girl. 'I never knew you could speak.'

'Well if you don't ask, you don't get,' said the cat. 'And if you don't look you don't see.'

'Look where?' asked the girl.

'Up the chimney of course,' said the cat.

So the girl did look and what did she see but a bag. A big bag. And when she got it down she saw it was full. Full of gold.

'I'd pick it up and run if I were you,' said the cat. So the girl grabbed the bag and put it on her back, and she ran out the house, across the garden, through the gate, and off fast as she could through the wood.

But just as she had gone the witch came home, and straight away she could smell something wrong. So she looked up the chimney and saw that the bag was stolen and since the girl had gone too, then she knew.

'Why didn't you scratch and stop her?' she asked the cat.

'She fed me,' said the cat. 'And you never do that.'

So the witch spat at her and ran outside. 'Garden, why didn't you tangle and trip her?'

'She dug me and cleared me and cared for me too. I never even get a glance from you.'

'Gate, why ever did you let her through?'

'She mended me and you never do.'

The witch kicked it, and ran on through the wood, screaming and swearing and sniffing out the trail. The girl was well ahead; she had reached the apple tree. But she heard the witch getting closer and closer; soon she would catch her up:

> Apple tree, Apple tree hide me, before the old witch can find me.
> If she do, she'll break my bones and bury me under the marble stones.
> Apple tree do hide me.

The tree bent down and scooped her up, and put her high up on its trunk.

Soon enough the witch came up. 'Apple tree, did you see, a girl as skinny can be? She looked and she took my long-tailed bag, and she's got my gold, she got all I had.'

'Yes,' said the tree, 'she ran off to the right.' So the witch chased after, down the path to the right, and the girl climbed down and went off to the left.

But by and by the witch saw she was tricked, and she turned and she ran the other way. Now the girl could hear her catching up again. Just then she saw the cow:

> Cow, oh Cow, do hide me, before the old witch can find me.
> If she do, she'll break my bones and bury me under the marble stones.
> Oh Cow, do hide me.

So the cow hid her in the long, long grass, under her swishing tail.

Sooner than ever, the witch was there. 'Cow, oh Cow, did you see, a girl as skinny can be? She looked and she took my long-tailed bag, and she's got my gold, she got all I had.'

'Yes,' said the cow, 'she ran off to the left.' So the witch chased after, down the path to the left, and the girl came out from under the cow's tail, and ran off to the right.

But by and by the witch saw she was tricked, and ran back the other way. Now the girl heard her almost at her heels:

Oven, oh Oven, do hide me, before the old witch can find me.

If she do, she'll break my bones and bury me under the marble stones.

Oven, do hide me.

'Very well,' said the oven, 'crouch behind me, but when the time comes be ready.'

The girl had hardly hidden herself before the witch was there. 'Oven, oh Oven, did you see, a girl as skinny can be? She looked and she took my long-tailed bag, and she's got my gold ...'

'Yes,' said the oven, 'look in me. She climbed inside to hide.'

So the witch opened the oven door, and reached right in, to grab the girl. But the oven gave a lurch and the girl gave a push, and then slammed the door shut, and that was that.

She thanked the oven, picked up the gold and danced all the way to the well. Spindle in the water, she went after, back home dry and safe. And weren't they surprised when she arrived with her great big bag of money! As there was so much, her father said she should have half, to do with as she wished.

The stepmother, of course, was none too pleased with this. But when she'd heard the whole tale through, she thought her own daughter should go too; for where there's money found, there's always hope of more.

So she sent her own child off to the well, telling her exactly what to do. This girl never even tried to spin; she just took her mother's spindle and threw it in. She didn't really want to jump in after, but her mother had told her it was not real water.

So in she leaped. But the well was deep, and the water was wet, and she couldn't swim, so down she went.

When her daughter did not come home, the mother went to the well to see where she had gone. Some say she slipped. Some say she jumped. All say she went in and never came up.

So the girl and her father were left by themselves. And with riches aplenty they lived very well.

8

GILBERT BECKET'S CRUSADE

Gilbert Becket was a mercer, not a knight. He knew all about trading cloth, especially silk, but he didn't know how to fight. Nor would he, normally, have wanted to.

But a call had come from Pope Urban that the Holy Lands must be saved from the Infidel, and all lords of Christendom should leave local strife and unite in a new Just War. 'God Wills It', the word went out; '*Deus volt*', the Crusader's cry. All must 'take the cross' and make himself a 'soldier of the Church.'

Europe was whipped into a frenzy of fervour, princes and barons excited by promises of feudal fiefdoms, soldiers by dreams of rich pickings, and traders and travellers by hopes of safer shipping routes. Even pilgrims, who had always been guaranteed safe passage by Muslim rulers, were swayed by the spread of stories of massacres now taking place. But the deciding factors for many were the Papal promises. Indulgences for all participants; however sinful, they would go straight to heaven if they died. And financial incentives like the waiving of all debts for three years. A huge lure, since everyone assumed the Crusades could be done in one.

It was this that drew Gilbert. He had just paid his issue fees, having finished his apprenticeship, and he was setting up his own business. Although he came from a wealthy mercer family, he wanted to stand on his own two feet. So he had borrowed a large amount from a money lender near the London Stone. Good rates, though high interest and punishing penalty clauses for default. Those didn't worry Gilbert, because he knew the silk trade was booming. And with three years without interest he might even clear his debts!

Besides, as his father pointed out, travel was good for traders. 'It could be a chance to make personal contacts in some of the cities you pass through. Venice, of course, but also Ragusa, and maybe, even Jerusalem itself!' he boomed enthusiastically. And if Old Becket was behind an idea, it was bound to be a sound one.

The less sound reasons for leaving home, Gilbert kept to himself. He had no need of Papal indulgences because his peccadilloes were so minor, easily absolved at no great cost. Ever since he was fourteen he had kept his head down, doing nothing but work, learning his trade. And throughout this last year all he could hear was talk, talk, talk of the Holy War – the excitement and fun, and the glory to be won. Gilbert was young, and before he settled down he wanted a taste of the free life of a knight!

He wasn't the only one. His servant, Richard, whom he had known ever since he was born, was as boyishly eager as he was. They took the Cross together, making their vows as a pilgrim would, and joined a Norman baron's entourage, setting off at once for France.

Their first shock was the crossing. Neither had been in a ship before, and the sea was rough. So was the lifestyle once they arrived in France. Nothing was as Gilbert had imagined. Disgusted by the food, the sleeping quarters and the lack of washing facilities, and exhausted by army training and daily drills, he might not have managed at all if not for Richard, who was well-used to physical work, and eating whatever you got. Richard also had an endless store of jokes and anecdotes to cheer his master up, and that soon won them other friends.

Slowly, as they travelled on, through France and into Italy, life improved. Although the journey was exhausting, the weather was good, and when people saw the crosses on their clothes and shields, many gave them fresh water, or little gifts of fruit.

So at last they came to the great port of Venice. Gilbert was impressed, all the more so because here he stayed with a friend of his father's, rediscovering his delight in comfortable and civilised company. Fine food, rich red wine, exquisite music, and before he left a purse of money, at his father's request, to improve his travelling fund.

Richard, ever practical, insisted on sewing most of it into the breasts of both their tunics, hidden underneath the cross.

The passage on along the Balkan coast was even worse than their first boat, for now it had got hot. For Gilbert, Ragusa alone stood out, like a single picture burnt on the mind in a fiery fever, yet one he could never have conjured up for himself.

A walled city like London, hanging on the sea as London clung to the Thames. A city of many faces from many different places.

'But there,' he thought, 'comparison ends, for here the range of differences endlessly extends.' Traders from the four corners of the world; strings of mysterious eastern spices, men with skin as dark as night, walrus tusks from lands of ice, silk far finer than he had ever seen, signs and scripts he could never read. And the people themselves, and the languages they spoke – bubbling, barking, some semi-singing, and some sounding half-caught in the throat. Gilbert had never supposed such variety could exist, let alone all be held in one small walled city. 'Oh!' he said to Richard. 'Think if London were like this!'

Gilbert himself thought of little else, holding the memory in his mind like a talisman to keep away the horrors of the endless voyage. People crying and dying, sickness, and the stench of it everywhere. And salt in the mouth, on the lips, and even crusting round the eyes. Until the longed-for morning, when all at once, it seemed to him, they arrived.

Constantinople. And the news came as they disembarked. They were late, and the main force had already gone on to Jerusalem. As soon as they were ready and fit to march, they were to go to Tyre. And yet before they were either, they were hurried on their way. Onwards now through regions that Crusaders had won.

And now Gilbert and Richard had their first taste of war. So much confusion: messages back and forth, factions fighting over stores of food and drink, and arguments arising from old feuds. All the rivalries of Europe, especially France, since most of the Crusaders there were Franks, were re-emerging now under the pitiless Saracen sun.

As they came closer to Jerusalem, news filtered back. At first triumphant announcements, then an undercurrent of whispers.

Jerusalem was taken, it seemed. A wondrous victory claimed. Some said the 'soldiers of the Church' had only had to pray, and the walls fell down. Others thought it had not been defended. Still others said the city had surrendered. 'But if so,' whispered some, 'why was half the city burned? Why did all the children and women also die?' The answers were hinted in the ashes of the still-smoking villages they passed – the eyes of any left behind, who ran to hide at the sight of soldiers marching by. Or worse, the ones who could not run, and simply lay, their awful injuries on full display.

Gilbert tried not to see, nor think too much. It was not hard. They were so tired. And so many of their soldiers were ill. '*Deus volt*' – 'As God Wills'. Maybe Tyre would simply open its gates, and welcome them as friends. And then their Just and Holy War could end for them, before it even wholly began.

As it turned out, his hopes were no more foolish than their leader's expectations. For assuming that Tyre, like Jerusalem, had only their inhabitants to defend them, they attacked openly, without much strategy. To their surprise, they found themselves facing Zahir al-Din, the Muslim leader of Damascus, who was also fighting in God's name. Having heard of the massacres at Jerusalem, he had answered Tyre's appeal for defence.

Even the best-laid plans would not have helped Gilbert or Richard. Barely knowing which direction they were supposed to be fighting in, they were caught trapped against the city walls. Luckily for them, they surrendered to an eminent amir, a prince who observed the code of Islam and the rules of war, never to harm a man who has yielded to you. Besides, from the way Gilbert spoke and behaved, it was clear that he was well born, and would be worthy of a good ransom. And he was so concerned about his friend, it was assumed that he must be more than a mere servant.

So both were taken prisoners, and word was sent to London that they would be released once the ransom was paid. And meanwhile they were treated according to their station with all due courtesy and respect. They were housed in spacious and comfortable rooms, and although, of course, they were not free to leave, they soon found the amir's palace a pleasant place to be.

Confident that the ransom would soon be paid, Gilbert settled down to make the most of his stay. Looking round, with the eyes of a trader, he saw so much he could learn from. The carpets were remarkable, for a start. Such intricate patterns, all woven in fine silk. He wondered if there was anyone he could talk to about them. Some of the servants spoke some French, but not enough. Gilbert had an interest in languages, and a willingness to work at them, and so he began to try to master Arabic.

The amir was amused by this, and after a while impressed. He began to call for Gilbert to come and talk to him, and the more he did, the more he liked him. Soon the young man felt almost like a guest. He began to eat at the amir's table, and spend evenings listening to music with him, being introduced to new instruments and ways of playing. It reminded him of staying with his father's friend in Venice.

And at the request of the amir, he told him in exchange about life in London. Sometimes he grew homesick as he talked, describing the Thames in all its moods, or an occasional nightingale singing in the evening. But neither man knew someone else was listening.

The women's quarters had a room adjoining the music hall. It was separated by a fine lattice-work wall, intricately patterned so the holes were almost invisible.

Equally well hidden, the amir's wives and daughters on the other side of the wall were free to come and go as they pleased, listening to the concerts so often played below. And here the youngest of his daughters had lately taken to stealing in on her own. At first she went simply to hear the music her father chose for his new guest. But lately she'd taken to lingering on, listening to the young man himself.

The amir was a wise and learned man, and prided himself on giving all his children – daughters, as well as sons – as wide an education as possible. But of all of them, it was his youngest daughter who had proved to be a scholar after his own heart. She had the desire to learn, and the mind to hold all that she was taught, and was as fluent as her father in several languages, including that of the Franks. She was thankful for this now, for that was the language the amir and his young friend most commonly used, although frequently making little forays into Arabic for Gilbert's sake. The amir's daughter loved to hear him struggling with her native tongue, making a myriad of amusing mistakes which her ever-patient father corrected one by one.

But most of all, she loved it when Gilbert told stories of his home. She could almost see the pale lacy green of an English spring, hear the rippling notes of the bird in the garden, and feel the icy wind through his City gates. And then one evening her father persuaded him to sing in his rough English language. It was like nothing she had ever heard before, and she fell in love with it, and with the singer too.

One morning, Gilbert was walking in the amir's garden. Past the sparkling fountains and through tall columns of flowers so fragrant that it almost made him faint. Through the grove of almond trees, heavy with nuts, which he could freely pick and eat. Then up through the waving palms towards a little stone building where he loved to sit, for it was always cool there. But as he climbed towards it, he heard the sweet sound of a young girl singing. Although he did not understand the words, the meaning of the song pierced him to the heart. Love, hopelessly longed for. And that was how he met the amir's daughter.

Days tuned into weeks, and they met, secretly snatching what moments they could, eyes understanding, hearts opening each to each, hands holding, lips finally meeting lips. And they, too, talked of everything and anything. As they did, little by little, impossibilities began to appear feasible, differences no longer so extreme. Even their beliefs, their Christian or their Moslem creed, when they discussed these deeply, no longer seemed so separate as to merit such great conflict. Why could they not unite, like two sides of the one coin, both part of the divinity of God above?

Weeks went into months, and so became a year. Twelve months and still no sign of Gilbert's ransom. No word from England that a letter had arrived – nothing. Now Gilbert and Richard talked late into the night, wondering what might have happened to the message sent. Surely it must have been lost along the way? If Gilbert's father had received it, he would certainly pay. Another thing was troubling Gilbert too. The time spent on the Crusade, and this year now with the amir, meant he was only free of debts for one more year. If he was not back by the end of that, and ready to pay some interest straight away, it could be called default. Then his creditor had the right to seize everything he had, his business and his goods, and all that he wished to take. Now, too late, he saw the mistake he had made in his agreement. What he did not know was that many creditors, angry at the debt-free laws imposed on them, were seizing any chance to prevent some crusaders from ever coming home from the Holy Land.

The amir's daughter was also worried. If the ransom did not come, her father could not let Gilbert go, much as he might wish to do so. Nor could he keep him for ever as his guest. Either way would be breaking the rules. The only honourable option, which he could not put off forever, would be to execute his prisoner, as an example to everyone else. She knew her father was concerned about this too, from the way he obliquely referred to the ransom in his evening conversations with Gilbert.

It was Richard who suggested the solution. They would have to escape, and make their own way back home. And that could only be done with the help of the amir's daughter. Gilbert did not want to ask, but she saw the question in his eyes, and wondered why she had not thought of it herself.

One moonless night when her father was with one of his wives, she stole the key, unlocked their door, and led them out to where she had two horses waiting, their hooves bound in cloth to silence them. 'Only promise me one thing,' she said as Gilbert held her in his arms one last time. 'When you are home and safe, then send for me.'

Gilbert gave her half the gold he had sewn underneath his cross. 'Take this,' he said to her, 'as my saddaq. My marriage gift to you. When you hear from me, use this gold to carry you home to England.'

Enough of rides, sea voyages and adventures. Suffice to say at long, long last, Gilbert and Richard arrived back safe in London. What a welcome they had there! And when they were done with the celebrations, the stories and the explanations, the exclamations and expostulations, and when even his mother had stopped sobbing with relief, then Gilbert tried to decide how to send a message to the amir's daughter. But now it seemed so hard. She was so far, far away. And he didn't know what to say that would not give her away, for having some connection or part in their escape. Whatever he said might endanger her. The only way to keep her safe must be to seem to forsake her.

Far away across the sea, the amir's daughter waited in vain for news. For weeks, for months, for almost a whole year. Yet she refused to give up. She could not forget him.

And she knew he would not forget her. One evening her father called her. He wished to talk about a marriage proposal. She kissed his hands, and hoped he might forgive her one day.

Later that night she cut her hair as short as any boy, and tied a man's headscarf round it. She bound cloth tight across her breasts, and put on a short linen tunic, with baggy trousers below. Inside these she hid her money bag. Finally, she wrapped her oud in soft cloth to protect the strings, and around that an old cloak of her brothers, and then she slipped like a shadow out of the palace where she had lived all her life.

She rode until dawn, and then sold her horse, knowing she was not getting a good enough price for such a beautiful beast, but hoping that the man who bought it would keep it well hidden, for fear it was stolen. Around the corner she bought a nag that would do for a while, and so arrived at Constantinople, and the sea passage to Venice. Mostly she kept herself to herself on the ship, her oud held close but silent, as she stared out at the water endlessly.

But in Venice she met with a group of minstrels travelling in the right direction, and tagged along with them. Since she could play well, and had a sweet voice too, and asked for nothing but their company along the road, they were happy enough to have another boy in the troupe for a while, though she seemed strangely aloof from the others.

In France she paid for a ride to the port, and nearly had her oud stolen, and the passage to England took almost the last of her coins. The sea was grey and rough, but England was greyer and colder too. And it was the hardest place of all, for here she could hardly speak. She and Gilbert had spoken in French, so all she had learnt from him was snatches of songs. And people stared at her so. For the first time she was truly afraid. She paid for a cart ride to London in exchange for her oud. The last of her jihaz, she thought sadly; the end of her dowry. The carter had no idea what it was, but he saw from the wood and the workmanship that he would make some money from it. So he was inclined to be nice to this delicate little lad, help him out if he could. But the strange little creature did not even seem to know where he was going. 'London,' was all he could say. And 'Gilbert Beckett', which didn't make any sense at all. The carter did his best. He took his passenger across London Bridge, and pointed to the east; that seemed the most likely possibility for whatever it was the boy was after.

The amir's daughter wandered along by the city walls. At least she knew what they were. But she'd never expected London would be so big. She didn't know where to look. All she could do was ask passers-by for Gilbert; Gilbert Beckett.

It was Richard who heard the boys laughing outside the shop. He'd stepped out to get something to eat, but also, to be honest, to have a break from Gilbert. Much as he liked him – and he was more a friend than master now, after all the two had been through together – Gilbert was maddeningly miserable these days. And he had everything too, as far as Richard could see. The shop was doing well and all London was open to him – he'd even been invited to the court. Going on the Crusades had done nothing but good for his status as a mercer and a dashing young man. But all he could do was mope about the girl he had left behind. Some people didn't know when they were lucky!

But there was definitely something going on right then. Cheapside was always noisy, full of carts going past and traders' cries, but this was a different kind of shouting. Half the street was blocked by a tight ring of boys standing around someone, taunting and teasing. Then he heard an answering outburst from whoever was in the middle, a torrent of strange words, which he suddenly recognised as Arabic. And the voice? It was oddly familiar. He pushed his way through, just as she, like a badger at bay, swung around. Even disguised as a boy, he knew at once who she was.

So the amir's daughter found her Gilbert at last. And the two sides of the coin were united. She was christened before they were married in St Paul's, but although she joyously embraced her new life, she never lost her love and respect for the old. And when their son was born, both parents brought him up to recognise the best of both their worlds, East and West. They also taught him to be wise and see the evils on both sides.

Some say that is how their son, Thomas à Becket, grew up to be so just; and in the end he joined St Paul as patron saint of London. A place that was to be, like his father's dream of Ragusa, a centre for all people, all languages, and all creeds to come together.

There's space for us all
Say the bells of St Paul's

9

LEGENDS OF
THOMAS À BECKET

The likelihood of Thomas' mother finding Gilbert was so small that it was declared a miracle by the bishops of St Paul's. That such a marriage might last between a couple as alike as chalk and cheese was – according to London ladies – a miracle beyond belief.

And so a double miracle ensured that Thomas à Becket was born. A fitting start, you might say, for a saint. Go on as you begin. But Thomas wasn't looking for miracles; they were looking for him. He wasn't born a saint. He wasn't even a saintly child. He grew up like other young men, sometimes reckless and wild. And since he was wealthy, healthy and strong, he had more of those times than some.

But he was in good company there. Some might say the best. He had a friend, a youth a little younger than him, equally fond of hawking and hunting, equally ready to spare no expense in maintaining a state of magnificence. Equal in so many things. Some said they shared a single heart and mind. But there was one great difference. Thomas' friend was the king. Henry II of England, great-grandson of the Conqueror.

Thomas was Henry's Chancellor. Eloquent, loyal and wise. He had helped to put him onto the throne, and he gave him good advice. The two worked together on many good reforms. And the king's son was fostered out in Thomas à Becket's house. It was obvious to everyone the two were very close. And inevitably many in the court grew envious.

They resented Becket's lifestyle too. When he had to travel, he took hundreds in his retinue. Knights, squires, clerics, and 100 household servants, minstrels, poets, and entertainers of all sorts. But also kennelmen, falconers, huntsmen – with horses – hawks, hounds, and even monkeys. Some said the chancellor's entourage rivalled that of the king.

But Thomas had another side, which most of the court didn't see. For he was a cleric, a learned clergyman, practicing austerities, and, when he could, retreats. He'd begun at Merton Priory and, rising rapidly, was Archdeacon of Canterbury by the time he was thirty-six. And his charity was as generous as any royal gift. Many poor Londoners blessed him for it. If Thomas came to preach at the cathedral in Southwark, beggars blocked the bridge to watch when he came out. And the ferrymen would fight to ferry him across; they knew he remembered who each man was. He gave alms to everyone, and prayed for them too. Couldn't ask for more than that from anyone, could you?

Sometimes Thomas wondered how it came to be, that he seemed to be split between two different worlds. Was it just what his parents taught him? Or maybe it was due to his name. Thomas means 'twin', but there was only one of him. Perhaps he was two men inside one skin. But there was no conflict between them. King and Church, he could serve both, equally devotedly.

Until Theobald, Archbishop of Canterbury, the head of the Church in England, died. And then Henry asked his friend to take up this position. However much Thomas refused, the king wouldn't listen, even when Thomas tried to explain that this would put them in opposition. 'You would require of me what I could not agree to,' he said. 'Then the envious would make strife between us.' But Henry could not understand why things between them would have to change.

To clear the air and restore high spirits, they went, as always, out hawking. It was a clear day and as they rode along beside the river, Thomas caught a glimpse of himself reflected in the water. Close behind his king, with his leather-clad arm raised, falcon on his wrist, he remembered with a wry smile a comment a fellow clergymen had said to him once: 'You look more like a falconer than a cleric.'

At that moment three ducks flew overhead, and both men turned and loosed their hawks, watching them fly, climbing the sky. Both were after the leader duck, Thomas' slightly ahead. 'You have the better of me, my friend,' the king said. But as Thomas' falcon swooped, the duck plunged down towards the river, and with the bird of prey hard on its tail, it dived. Too late to stop itself, the falcon hit the water, and unable to swim or rise again, it was swept away before their eyes.

Without a moment's hesitation Thomas leapt in after, but the current was stronger than he expected. The king called out in horror, but was unable to help him. Thomas caught his hawk and managed to throw it free up into the air, but he himself was dragged away by the river. He was able to keep himself upright, and swim after a fashion, but could not get to the bank on either side. And it was then that he remembered the mill. It was only half a mile downstream. If he could not get out before then, he would surely be caught in the wheel. But hard though he tried, it was hopeless. He could only accept the inevitable, and give himself up to God above. There was even a feeling of relief as he closed his eyes.

Just before the mill there was a bend in the river. The water was swirling, already caught in the race. But as he turned the curve Thomas sensed it slow, circling on itself, stilling, suddenly sluggish. Looking up, he saw the king hurrying to the mill, just as the miller, shaking his head, came out to meet him. Catching sight of Thomas then, the man ran instead for a pole and, grabbing hold of it gratefully, Thomas was brought to dry land.

'Well, there is a lucky man,' the miller said. 'Though how and why it happened, I cannot say.'

'At least you managed to stop the mill in time,' said Thomas. 'That was quick work.'

'But I didn't,' said the miller, scratching his head. 'It was an accident. The wheel just stopped.'

The message to Thomas was clear. If it was time for him to choose one side or the other, then he knew what he must decide. He was in God's hands. And so when the Pope's legate overrode his scruples, he accepted his lot, and became the Archbishop of Canterbury.

Then Thomas went into his cathedral, and took off the jewels and silk clothes of the court, and put on a plain linen surplice and rough cloth cassock. As he did so, he thought of his mother, and how she too had dressed anew when she moved from one life to the other: Damascus to London. Two sides of the same coin. Would that be true for him too? He hoped it would prove so. But he had few illusions. Now he would be answerable to the Pope, his master, over and above his friend, the king. Whether or not that would cause conflict was not up to him, but if it did so, he would have to stand firm. To strengthen his resolve, beneath his cleric's clothes, he now put on a hair shirt, to remind his skin of the man who was within. But he also took his mother's crescent moon, a golden scimitar, to remind him of her, and the joyous resolution that she found. And this he hung over the high altar of Canterbury Cathedral. They say, too, that as he spent his first night there, in solitary vigil and prayer, the Virgin Mary came to visit him. In the morning, when she'd gone, as proof that she had been she left him the Golden Eagle Ampulla, to hold the oil for royal coronations ever after.

But despite these comforts, it turned out as Thomas feared. For Henry wished to strengthen the powers of the State, and that pressed hard against the powers of the Church. It seemed to Thomas that the games of chess, which he and Henry had enjoyed playing together at court were now fought out in real life. First came the struggle over payment of landowners' tax; and then over clerics' right to choose ecclesiastic trial. The first, played on a board, might have called on knights and castles; the second on the full force of the bishops and the Queen. Money and laws; quarrels lead to wars – as Thomas knew only too well. The issues could not be resolved and Henry was furious that Thomas should so obstinately support the Church against him. He exiled him, and Thomas went to Rome, and the Pope.

Arriving at the Apostolic Lateran Palace after a very long journey, Thomas was hungry. Expecting the Pope to send for him at once, he called for food to be brought quickly and, since it was a fast day, he asked for carp, which, being fish, was permitted. Instead, in an attempt to discredit him, he was served a capon just as the Pope's messengers arrived to collect him. Deeply shocked by his behaviour, they insisted on taking the bird as well as Thomas straight to the Pope. But on arrival, when they took the lid off the dish, they found the capon had turned into a fish.

But minor miracles could not protect Thomas forever. At the Pope's request he was allowed to return from exile, but again refused to give into Henry's demands. 'Oh who will rid me of this troublesome priest?' the king exclaimed in an outburst of hurt rage, and so set the stage for the end. Four knights were ready to take him at his word, and made their way to Canterbury immediately. And although Becket received letters of warning, he refused to allow the cathedral to be locked against any who wished to enter.

It was twilight and vespers were being sung. As Thomas came into the cathedral, the king's knights, strongly armed, came behind. 'Away, you cowards,' Becket said calmly, pointing to their weapons. 'A church is not a castle.' He went towards the choir, and a monk, Edward Grim, stood beside him. The knights pushed after them.

'Where is Thomas the traitor?' they shouted.

'Here I am,' he replied, coming down the steps to stand between the altars. 'No traitor, but archbishop and priest of God. I am ready to die, but God's curse on you if you harm my people.'

Fitzurse struck first, then Tracy. Grim intercepted the blow with his own arm, but it forced Thomas to his knees, and blood ran down into his eyes. 'Into Thy hands, O Lord,' he cried, 'I commend my spirit!' Le Bret struck deep into his head, breaking his sword against the pavement, and Hugh of Horsea added the final blow.

'Let us away,' he cried, 'this man will rise no more.' Red blood, white with brain, stained the floor of the cathedral, and marked the footsteps of the knights as they ran out. A thunderstorm broke in full fury overhead.

Trying to run from the sky itself, the murderers hurried to a manor house nearby. As they went in they threw their weapons on a table in the hall. But the table trembled from the touch of this awful burden, and then violently hurled it all to the floor. And when they ate and threw their scraps and bones to the dogs, they curled their lips and slunk away, refusing to take food from such bloodied hands. And so they went from place to place, to try to hide. But there was no escape for they were excommunicated, and the curse of the Pope followed them, on land, sea and air, above, below and everywhere.

As for the king, when the news came to him, he knew his own words had killed his best friend. He shut himself away, and fasted for forty days. Later he was absolved by the Pope. But many never forgave him, including his own son, who had felt more love from Thomas in one day, he said, than his father had given him all his life.

Thomas à Becket was hailed as a holy martyr, and the Pope had a requiem mass said for him. Within three years he was canonised, and became a patron saint of London on a par with St Paul. On London Bridge, where the beggars used to wait for him, a chapel was built in his memory, and all who came to London went there first to give thanks for a safe journey.

The old Roman road from London Bridge to Canterbury soon became known as the 'Pilgrim's Way'. And St Thomas à Becket's tomb was covered with gold, silver, and jewels, and became famous for its many miracles. The blood from his head that spilt upon the floor was wiped up by the monks and laymen. One of these men took a bloodied cloth home to his sick wife, and she was instantly well again. Then the cloths were used for everyone, and the blood was watered down to make healing water, and hundreds reported cures from it. Adam the Forester was shot in the throat by a poacher, but drank the holy water of St Thomas and was healed. Hugh the cellarer was receiving the Last Rites, but the water restored him to life.

Many did not even need the water. Jordan of Plumstead, who had served Thomas in London, prayed to him to help his daughter who had wasted right away. St Thomas took pity on her, and she sat up in her bier whole and well. While William the carpenter, who cut his leg with an axe, dreamt of St Thomas and, when his bandages were taken off, found there was no wound there at all. To this day his healing powers are remembered in the naming of south London's St Thomas Hospital, close to the place where he once gave alms to all, after his sermons at Southwark Cathedral.

Nearby in Lambeth Palace, the London residence of the Archbishop of Canterbury, built soon after Thomas died, they put St Thomas' statue in the Water Tower. It was facing the river, so the ferrymen could salute him, which they did whenever they passed. Even today, though the statue is long gone, the boatmen doff their caps there.

10

BLIND BEGGAR'S DAUGHTER

Rags make paper
Paper makes money
Money makes rulers
Rulers make wars
Wars make want
Want makes beggars
Beggars make rags …

There was a time, and it wasn't my time, and it wasn't your time, but it was in hard and hungry times when London town had beggars whichever way you turned. Even if you wandered out to pleasant villages round about, such as Bethen Hall Green, to the east, with its ponds and mansion houses and trees, and sense of leisurely ease, there were still more seeking alms than there were almshouses to dispense them. Although the strong and handsome Edward 'Longshanks' was on the throne, there had been many troubled years before when England had been split by civil war – barons against their liege lord, cousin against cousin, even godfathers in mortal combat with their own godsons. And afterwards, though peace had come, the country was still carrying its scars. So the lamed and maimed, the homeless, widowed, orphaned, old, and young, were beggars all, though they held nothing in common but their want.

Yet amongst the crowd some did stand out. And one such man lived quietly in Bethen Hall Green. He was old, blind, ragged and thin, he was certainly poor, and yet he had a gentleness about him that made people careful about how they spoke when he was about. Especially because he had a very beautiful daughter, with a clear sweet singing voice and a smile that melted everyone's heart. Her name was Bessie.

These two were always together, although it was clear sometimes that the old man was unhappy that his daughter should always be in such rough company. But whenever he suggested to her that she should try and find a better situation for herself, she would just laugh, and shake her head. For she could never leave him to fend for himself.

One day the old blind beggar heard the sound of something whining pitifully, and sent Bessie hurrying off to see what the trouble was. She soon found a poor bitch which had had a litter of puppies in the ditch, but being too weak and thin, she was unable to feed them. One of the pups was whimpering, and trying to clamber out. The girl picked it up and took it to her father, and he found a scrap of whey cheese he had been given, and fed the little creature crumb by crumb. From that day on, the puppy loved the old man so much that he followed him everywhere, and looked after him in every way he could. And because he was quick and clever, Bessie's father taught him all sorts of tricks, and that delighted passers-by, who would stop, and pay a coin or two to watch the fun. He was also presented with a bell, so that people would know when he was coming, and pay attention when he was crossing the road. In this way, the blind beggarman became well known, and people would watch out for him.

Seeing this, Bessie began to feel that the time had come when she might happily leave him more often on his own, so when he asked her again to try to find some other kind of occupation for herself, she agreed. But hoping to find honest work, she turned her back on London town and walked instead through marshy ground towards the North.

She had walked for a day or two, and was getting very tired, when, in the village of Romford, she came to a coaching inn named after the king. There she stopped to rest, and begged for a piece of bread to eat.

'I have no coins to pay, but I'll work in exchange – a good full day,' she said. The innkeeper's wife took her at her word, but once she had seen how hard the girl worked, she said a half day was enough, and gave Bessie a good meal too.

At that Bessie felt bold enough to ask if she might stay on as a tavern wench, and the landlady agreed, for she knew so pretty a girl would help bring people in. Especially when she heard Bessie could sing. But she was a good woman at heart, and warned the girl that she might find some of the customers a little rough. At which young Bessie threw back her head and laughed.

'My father is a London beggarman,' she said. 'Although an honester one you will never find. So I have had practise aplenty in dealing with men of all kinds.'

So, Bessie stayed, and in no time the innkeeper's wife was treating her like a daughter. And the young men were coming like bees to blossom. And when they heard sweet Bessie sing they lost their hearts altogether. The good wife, taking the girl's affairs to heart, was careful to stress that she was not to be trifled with; 'marriage or nothing,' she said. And seeing that amongst the suitors was a knight, a rich man's son, and a merchant who was also well-to-do, she also took Bessie aside. 'Watch what you say my girl,' she said, 'you could end up some rich man's bride.'

Imagine how dismayed she was when the girl received all offers with the same words, 'First ask my father for consent. He's known at Bethen Hall Green. He is the blind beggar with the dog and bell, who daily sits begging for charity.'

'That's it,' sighed the innkeeper's wife. 'You won't see them for dust.' And indeed the merchant and the rich man's son, and many others too, were soon gone.

But the knight remained. 'It is yourself, and not your purse I love,' he said. 'I will gladly ask your father, if you will give me hope.'

'More than that,' she said joyfully, 'for if you wish, I will come now with you.' And so Bessie retraced her steps, but this time sat upon a horse, with her true love beside.

Gossip, however, goes faster than horse's hooves, and the knight's family were outraged to hear that he meant to marry a penniless beggar's daughter. When they arrived at Bethen Hall Green, Bessie's father was surrounded by the knight's brothers, armed and angry, and beggars from all over town who had gathered to take Bessie's part if need be.

They all stepped back to make a circle round the three, and Bessie helped her father to his feet. Knight faced beggar, and each held out their hand to the other.

'But if it is money that you rate,' the blind man cried, 'let us turn and turnabout, drop down an angel for the bride. My gold, I'm sure, will more than equal yours.'

For every coin the knight and his kinsmen threw down, the beggar tossed two more upon the ground. And on and on it went until the knight's gold was all spent, and the beggar's daughter's bridal gift was £30,000.

'And now I'm free,' her father said, 'by "Longshanks" leave to say. My daughter is far better born than many noble men. I lost my sight in battle, and my father in the same. Evesham was the battle, de Montfort was his name.'

So the truth came out, and all was reconciled on every side. Bessie fairly won her man, and he his honest bride.

And many a toast to both was drunk at the inn where they both met:

Then take her and make her your jewel so bright,

For many a lord this wedding would spite,

The most beautiful damsel that ever was seen,

The blind beggar's daughter of Bethen Hall Green.

If you fancy raising a glass too, on behalf of love, or luck, or ballads about them, you could always try the Blind Beggar's pub on Whitechapel Road. Though I don't think they accept angels any more.

11

DICK WHITTINGTON

There's many a slip betwixt cup and lip.
Maybe that led to the tale of poor Dick.
For some say the story began with Sir William of Pauntley's
youngest son
Whose name was Richard Whittington.

However it started, however he came from Gloucestershire to London town, on the back of a horse or the flat of his foot, along the way, he lost half his name. Take the 'rich' from Richard, and you're left with only 'hard' and that indeed is how his new life went. For London town was a hard place for a country boy to establish himself; whether he be an orphan, or just the youngest son, heir to nothing but hope.

As he grew closer to London, the road he was on met up with others, until it seemed that all the roads in the world were leading in the same direction. And more and more traffic joined him too, from every side, until he felt he was being carried along on a river of travellers of all kinds. There were carriages calling for room to pass, men on horseback, donkey carts, people driving cows and sheep, one woman leading a line of geese, children running here and there, beggars begging everywhere.

Dick didn't know which way to look, until suddenly they emerged through woods onto open heath, and there beneath were the City walls and a great arched gate. High Gate – the north 'door' to London town.

People poured through like water flooding in, and as the road sloped down it seemed to him they were going faster and faster.

So many buildings of every shape and size! In the end he just wanted to shut his eyes, and open them to find himself at home again. Churches, arches, markets, houses, halls, away in the distance he thought he spied St Paul's. And the roads flowed into lanes, and alleys, and cuts and streets, some paved, too, though none with gold as he had been told they would be.

More swept along than choosing his own way, he found himself at last at London Bridge. There was a great stone tower at his end of it. And beyond that he could see shops built on the bridge, and houses too. There was even a chapel there, he knew, dedicated to St Thomas à Becket. He promised himself that as soon as he'd found his feet, he'd visit it.

But meanwhile he had to find the house where he was to stay, although how anything could be found in a city this size was beyond him.

Just then a young man not much older than him came strolling by. 'Are you alright?' he asked, with a smile. 'You look a bit lost.'

'Well yes I am,' said Dick, surprised and delighted to find someone so friendly at just the right moment. 'I'm looking for a house near London Stone.'

'Well that's the easiest place to find in the whole of London!' laughed the boy. 'You must be from far away if you don't know where it is. Come on, I'll take you, it's only a step or two down the river.'

So off they went together at great speed, and in no time at all young Dick had told his new friend all about himself. In return he heard so much about London ways, all rattled off at such a pace, that his head was whirling and he was quite out of breath with trying to keep up with it all.

It was certainly a good deal more than a couple of steps, but at last his friend stopped abruptly at a crossroads, and, catching hold of Dick's arm, he whirled him round about. 'Here you are! London Stone!' he cried, pointing to a huge slab, taller than a man. 'Can't miss it.' And indeed you couldn't, for it jutted so far into the street that barrows and carts had to trundle right round to pass.

'Now I must be off!' the young man said, and away he went with a cheery wave, before Dick had time to blink. 'Oh thank you!' he called. 'I'm most obliged.'

'Much obliged meself,' his friend answered with a laugh, as he disappeared round the corner. It was only when Dick was left alone, and he put his hand in his bag to get his papers and everything ready, that he realised why his friend had laughed so much and had been so obliged. For all that he'd possessed had gone: his purse; his apprentice papers; and even his little luck piece from home.

He turned, and ran a few steps after the boy. But it was hopeless. The thief had already vanished. Cursing himself for being a fool, and wavering between rage and tears, Dick wondered what to do next. He wouldn't ask anyone else for directions, anyway. There was no one to trust. So he wandered around, hoping he would find the house by accident. Instead he got lost, and soon it grew dark. He spent that night cowering in doorways, jumping up at any sound, and moving on if anyone came past. At dawn he made his way down to the river, hoping at least to wash his face, and drink a mouthful or two.

To his surprise when he got there, by the side of the tower, he saw a dozen or so boys, some his age, some younger, splashing at the water's edge. Keeping his distance, he was about to duck his head in, when one of them shouted 'Not there! Upstream!' and jerked his thumb eastwards. 'And watch it! Ain't safe to get in!'

Now he saw what they were doing. Washing skins. And the blood and mess was flowing his way. He called his thanks and went the other side of them. Here the river looked cleaner, but as soon as he dipped his hands in, he could feel the current pulling, and he understood what the boy meant. When he'd washed, he went over to thank him again.

'Deadly,' the lad agreed. 'When river's high someone always gets drowned. And when it's cold we freeze. Can't win, can you?' He sniffed and dragged an armful of soggy ram skins out onto the bank. 'Still, won't be forever, I'll get on to something better. If I survive, that is. I'm a 'prentice with the leather. We all start with this.'

Dick told him he was hoping to be an apprentice too, and the boy grinned. 'Good luck to you!' he said, and pointed the way back to the London Stone. And this time Dick was luckier, both in his choice of friends and in finding his way. For just as he saw the stone up ahead, he noticed a grand house on his right, with a picture outside that showed a Maid's Head, the sign of the mercer. It was surely the house he was looking for, and, as if in confirmation, he heard the familiar song of a blackbird calling to him from the garden behind. As soon as Cheapside stirred properly into life, Dick marched boldly across the street, and knocked on the door of the mercer, Mr Fitzwaryn.

It was opened by a maid, who looked him up and down and seeing how rough he looked by now, took him for a beggar. Shaking her head, she directed him to another entrance at the side of the house. When Dick knocked there, the door opened onto the warmth and rich smells of the kitchen, and the poor boy realised how hungry he was. But now it was the cook standing there glaring at him. 'What do you think you're after?' she cried. 'Coming here knocking as bold as the master!'

When Dick tried to explain, she picked up a skillet and chased him away.

As luck would have it, however, Mr Fitzwaryn came out at just at that moment, and although he was surprised to see Dick hovering near the door, all mud-spattered and forlorn, and without purse or letters or anything, he soon took charge of the situation, and brought him into the house.

So that was how Dick Whittington began his life as a loyal and obedient servant, and the newest and youngest apprentice to the merchant trade of the London Livery Company of Mercers. The 'Livery' part of the title had only just been introduced – on account of the elegant ceremonial robes that King Edward III encouraged guild members to adopt. The practical reason was that it helped show which guild was which, but the delight in such sumptuous clothing was also a sign of the times, amongst rich Londoners especially.

The mercers were general merchants, specialising in cloth, mostly exporting wool, and importing silk or linen or calico. Mr Fitzwaryn was one of the wealthiest; he only imported silk and velvet, and dealt in specially embroidered work, which was highly fashionable and much in demand at court. He had a workshop where it was woven, and seamstresses who made it into clothes;

he also had a shop where it was sold, as well as dealers who took it all over England and Europe. So it was the best of places for a likely lad to learn.

Sometimes though, because Dick was new, and young too, and knew so little about London life, the older apprentices would tease him and play all manner of tricks on him. But by and large they were good-natured, and Dick was so cheerful and hard-working that they could not help but like him. Of course, as the newest one to join, he had all the worst jobs, the ones that everyone wanted to pass on to someone else. But there was nothing nearly as bad as the apprentices in the leather trade had.

As well as working in the shop, the apprentices helped serve in the master's house. Dick did most of this, because he also lived there. And the best of that, as far as he was concerned, was Mr Fitzwaryn's daughter. Her name was Alice, and she was nearly thirteen, a year younger than him. She was light and bright as a summer's day, with a quick smile and a kind word for everyone. And she liked to talk to Dick about the things that he knew most about – creatures of the countryside, especially birds. He could imitate their songs, and made her laugh by mimicking the way they moved, too. But above all, she loved the story of Dick and the blackbird calling on that first morning. They could have talked for hours, if they'd ever had the time.

For it was a busy life that Dick lived, early morning to late at night. And he would have been happy – even with a bedroom in the roof so small there was not room to stand or move about at all – had it not been for two things.

The first was the rats and mice who ran all over him at night, and nibbled whatever they could find, including poor Dick's clothes. He was forever trying to fight them off, and make good the mess they had made. But worse than that was the constant harassment he had from the cook. When she discovered that Dick was the new apprentice, instead of being apologetic for chasing him away on the first day, she seemed to blame him for the mistake she had made. From then on she made his life as miserable as she could. She complained the fires that he built were too smoky, said he took too long if she sent him to buy something, that he left the sweepings of silk everywhere, and anything else she could think of. But harder still were the things she said to him when nobody else was about. That he was a clumsy country fool, and that people laughed at how he dressed. And she'd seen the way he looked at Miss Alice, and how he tried to impress, but hadn't he guessed that Alice herself mocked him behind his back? Poor Dick would lie awake wondering if what she said was true. And if it was, it would break his heart, but what was he to do?

So the days turned into weeks, and the months became one year and then two, and then almost three. Dick was doing all and more that he was asked to do, and being bright, he quickly learnt the ins and outs of the mercer's craft. One day he pleased the master so much that he was given ten groats and an afternoon off, to go and enjoy himself at the May Day celebrations.

So Dick and the other apprentices went down to All Hallows church, and from there all the way to Billingsgate there were garlands and ribbons and stalls. So they watched the parades and laughed at the jesters, and joined in the dances too. Then they wandered along the stalls, but there were so many fine things, Dick couldn't make up his mind what to buy.

But by the time he got to Billingsgate he was ready to eat, so he spent four of his groats on oysters, which he'd never had before, and he thought them the best thing he'd ever tasted. When he'd done he licked his lips and looked around and what did he see but a cat, watching him with desperate eyes. Knowing what it was like to be hungry, and enjoying the pleasure of being wealthy enough to do what he wanted, Dick bought the poor creature a whole fish for herself. She wolfed it down, bones and all, and then she stuck to him all afternoon, and when he started off for home she followed after.

Then suddenly a rough-looking man blocked his way. 'Oi!' he bellowed. 'What you doing with my cat?'

'She isn't yours,' protested Dick. 'She's a stray.'

'Only since she's strayed away from me!' said the man, snatching her up by the scruff. 'If you want her, you'll have to pay.' The poor creature meowed so piteously that Dick couldn't see what else to do but hand over the last of his money. So all he brought back from the fair was a cat. And that he hid under his doublet and carried upstairs to his room.

But for the first time since he'd arrived in London, he slept the whole night through. For the cat made herself busy at once, catching the rats and the mice. So from that night on, the cat grew fat, and ceased to be wild, and Dick relaxed, and stopped being so tired. And both had a friend to rely on.

Not long after, Mr Fitzwaryn had a new shipment of wool and cloth to sell abroad. He was a fair man, and he was doing well, so he decided to let all his apprentices and the whole household have a chance to share in trading overseas. So he called everyone downstairs, and asked if they had anything to sell that they would like the captain to take with him to barter on their behalf. Everyone had something except for poor Dick. He had neither money nor goods to offer.

'Surely,' said the cook, 'you have something of your own.'

Dick could not bear to be made to look so poor in front of Alice. 'Of course I do,' he said. 'I have a cat.'

The other servants laughed, but Mr Fitzwaryn said, 'well if you wish, you may send that.' Dick did not really want to, but he didn't see how he could say no. And so, with tears in his eyes, he took his puss and gave it to the ship's captain.

From then on his life was even more miserable than before. Now he had no friendly cat to keep him company at night, and instead the hungry mice and rats came back to plague him again. And the cook teased him mercilessly, the more so because she soon saw how much it upset him to think of his cat lost far away at sea. 'You know what they've probably done,' she said. 'They'll have skinned her to make bagpipes, so she can yowl and they can dance. Sailors love to do that!'

Because he was so unhappy and was sleeping so badly, Dick started making mistakes at work as well. Now even Mr Fitzwaryn was getting cross with him. It was more than he could bear. He had failed on all sides. And so he decided to run away. Of course, he knew that apprentices were bound for seven years at least. If he broke that he could never come back. He would be banned from the trade, and worse still, he would never be able to become a citizen of London town. But then he heard Alice laughing with the cook about something, and in his sorry state he assumed it was about him. And that was the last straw.

It was All Hallows Eve, and the whole household was late at church. When they came home he did not sleep, and as soon as it was getting light, he crept out and began to walk north. He climbed the long hill towards Highgate, the city gate he had come through all those years before. He remembered that now, and how different London had seemed then. And all his hopes and dreams. All come to nothing in the end. Now he was so very tired. He stopped for a minute to rest on the milestone by the side of the road. Dawn was breaking and far away the six bells of Bow church began to ring out for All Hallows Day. Over and over they rang the same peal, and as he listened he could hear what they were saying:

Turn again Whittington, Lord Mayor of London.
Turn again Whittington, Lord Mayor of London.
Turn again Whittington, Lord Mayor of London. Once. Twice.
Thrice. Yes!

He stayed there until he was absolutely sure; Lord Mayor of London. Three times over. That's what the bells were telling him. He knew Bow Bells would never lie.

And so Dick Whittington went back to the mercer's house, and slipped inside while everyone was still fast asleep. And from then on, whenever things were hard to bear, he'd remember Highgate Hill, and imagine himself there.

Meanwhile, Dick's cat was having adventures of her own. The ship she was on had sailed past France, and Venice too, far beyond the lands of Christendom and along the Barbary Coast to a place where gold was as plentiful as dust. There the captain stopped to trade, and as the people of that land were so different from them, many came just to see the sailor men. And so delighted were they with the curious goods brought from the cold lands of the North that the king of the land invited the captain to feast with him in his palace.

There, all things were so splendid that the captain was dazzled. Fine food of every kind was brought for him to eat. But before they could finish, rats and mice appeared from all sides, and in no time at all they had gobbled up everything. The captain was shocked, and asked the king if he would like these creatures stopped.

'Certainly,' the king replied. He would give a great deal of riches to anyone who could do that for him.

The captain was pleased for he remembered poor Dick and his cat, which was still on board, and a great favourite with all the sailors as she was such a good ratter. He sent for her straightaway. Being hungry by now, having long since eaten all the vermin on-board ship, the cat was delighted to meet some more. In less time than it takes to tell, she had killed 100 rats and mice, and had a feast herself as well.

Now the king and all his people were so eager to buy the cat that the captain barely had to bargain to get a casket of gold and pearls worth a prince's ransom.

And so it was that when the ship returned at last to London, the price Dick got in exchange for his cat was worth more than all the ship's cargo put together. And when Mr Fitzwaryn heard that, although some advised him that it would be too much for so young a man, he insisted Dick should have it all, down to the very last groat. And Dick himself was so generous that he well repaid his master, the captain, and everyone else, even giving something to the cruel cook.

Now when Dick came to the end of his apprenticeship, he had no trouble finding the money to pay the issue fee which was required to make him a freeman. Becoming then a 'lowys' or 'bachelor', he was also in the happy position of having enough money to open up his own shop and to take on his own apprentices straight away. But even more important than that, perhaps, he now felt he had the right to beg Alice to be his wife – just as she was beginning to give up hope that he would ever ask!

Although his first beloved cat never came back, cats continued to feature in Dick's life. For as his mercer business grew, he began to consider dealing in other goods. One of these was coal. Looking for ways to transport it, Dick heard of coal barges nicknamed 'Black Cats'. 'Cats will do for me!' he said. 'We'll bring them down the River Lea.'

Nobody else had thought of this shortcut, so coal barges on that route were called the 'Black Cats of Whittington'. And these cats too made him rich. So much so that within ten years he was Sheriff of London, and soon after was made Lord Mayor.

True to the peal of the bells, he was Lord Mayor of London for a second and a third term, which also meant that he was first to be told of the monarch's death, and twice became then, temporarily, the Principal Officer in the Kingdom. But Londoners knew him more as the familiar figure in his glorious robes, waving from the golden Lord Mayor's coach, flanked on either side by the effigies of Gog and Magog, the Giant Defenders of the Realm.

Even as Lord Mayor, Richard Whittington never forgot what it was like to be poor in London. He passed a law to prevent apprentices having to wash animal skins in the Thames when it was too cold or wet. He created drinking fountains, where anyone could get clean water, drainage systems, and a public toilet too. He founded the Whittington Hospital, and funded St Bartholomew's and St Thomas', creating a special ward for unmarried mothers. He also rebuilt Newgate Prison.

When he died, he was buried with his wife in his church, St Michael Paternoster.

> Here lies Sir Richard Whittington, thrice Mayor
> And his dear wife, a virtuous loving pair.
> Him fortune raised to be beloved and great
> By the adventure only of a cat.

His tomb is now lost, but a mummified cat was found in the church tower in the 1940s. And on Highgate Hill you can see still the Whittington milestone marker. Sit there and perhaps you'll hear the bells of Bow ring out for you too.

12

Ghosts in Good Company

The place in London most ridden with ghost stories is surely the Tower. There are boxfuls of them. For me the saddest tale is the one about the two princes, imprisoned by their uncle Richard III, and presumed murdered there – a theory borne out by the discovery of the bones of two boys secreted underneath the stairs of the Bloody Tower.

I was therefore pleased to hear, from a friend who knows Beefeaters at the Tower, that one of them saw two young boys, who he thought might be the princes, playing on the green, one evening.

I was even more pleased to hear this second story from her:

> A warden at Wakefield Tower has a young son, and he was looking for him one day, but couldn't see him anywhere. Eventually he found him in the Bloody Tower. 'What on earth were you doing in there?' he asked.

'I'm just talking to my friends,' the boy said. But it was after hours, the Tower was empty, so of course the warden was taken aback.

'What friends are they?' he wondered.

'The two boys who live here,' his son explained.

From his description they must have been the princes – ghosts maybe, but still playing happily with each new generation of friends.

13

St Uncumber's Shoes

When I was a bachelor I lived by myself
And all the bread and cheese I got I put upon the shelf.
But the rats and the mice they made such a strife
I had to go to London to buy myself a wife.

He might have done that, but she, on the other hand, might have come to London to lose herself a husband. And where could she do that? Why, Old St Paul's of course, at the shrine of the Maid, St Uncumber. Some folk had fancier names for her, like Wilgefort and Dignefortis, Reginfleid and Liberata. But whatever her name, she was the one women called on, when they needed a bit of help in unencumbering themselves.

If ye cannot sleep nor slumber
Give oats unto Saint Uncumber.

It hadn't been so easy for her, way back whenever it was that she'd been young, resisting some persisting pagan prince. She'd had to grow a beard to put him off, a big bristly, bushy one right down to her knees, and as if that wasn't uncomfortable enough, she was crucified as well.

But by the Middle Ages – well, people prided themselves on being a bit more civilised – all you had to do was to select the right saint and pray. And then – naturally – pay.

Some gave the Maid Uncumber gold, some gave her silver, some gave her wild oats and nightly thanks forever. It all depended on the size of the purses and the results of the pleas. They must have been successful by and large, because, by the time my story starts, her effigy was encrusted with coins, her beard studded with silver and her little wooden feet encased in solid gold shoes.

Golden Shoes! What a wonderful sight! To most people in London at that time, any kind of shoe was a sign of wealth. Plenty went without, inside and out cold soles slipping on the cobble stones. And such a one was a young musician come up to town for Bartholomew's Fair. He did well enough while it was there, but he'd stayed on once it was gone, fiddle under his arm all battered and worn, tunic and hose all tattered and torn, and nothing to keep him going now but the wind at his back and the hope in his heart. If hopes were horses we'd all ride high! But he was walking; round and round and round. Billingsgate to Bishopsgate and back, playing for scraps – and fighting for them, too. Then there were the nights snatching brief respite in doorways, with dogs and draughts and one eye always out for the Watch. And on this particular day it was just beginning to snow.

Our wandering fiddler lad, wondering where to go, found his bare feet had stopped on the steps of Old St Paul's. Inside was dry

and dim, infinitely welcoming: the smell of incense on the air, and the gentle murmuring of prayer. Timidly he tiptoed in. No one seemed to notice him.

In the flickering light of the tapers, shrines of saints stood side by side. The fiddler went to St Uncumber's; it seemed to him that her face was kind. As he sank down to the ground he saw wild oats piled round her feet, and, delirious with hunger, snatched them and began to eat. Only when he'd swallowed them down did he realise what he'd done. Stealing from a Holy Shrine! Sacrilegious capital crime! On his knees he begged forgiveness, and tried to think of ways to pay. All he had to give was music. Would that satisfy the Maid?

Gently he took up his fiddle, and with heart and soul he played. Shoulders hunched, head bowed, he was anxious at first, afraid his sort of music would not be allowed in this awesome, sacred place. But as his fingers stroked the strings a song of thanks rose up in him, and found its voice in the violin. And as it flowed, the music rose, soared like a bird, and hung, divine, wreathing the statue, filling the shrine. Feeling its strength, the boy stood straight, and for the first time raised his eyes to the saint. Surely she had heard.

He scarcely saw the shining silver of her clothing, nor the gleaming golden shoes. He was looking at her face, carved so carefully out of wood. The eyes ... the cheeks ... the chin ... the lips ... they almost seemed alive.

And as he looked – yes! He was right. The mouth twitched, and she smiled.

Weak with relief, he played a tune so sweet that now he made the lady sigh, and caught a crystal tear from her painted eye. Then with a laugh he bent back to his task with a lilting, rhythmic courtly dance. And as he did, her body too began to quiver and tremble and – so gracefully – to move. Now he drew his bow so fast that the music almost laughed and her toes began to tap and her feet began to dance, 'til she kicked out all at once – and a shoe fell in his lap.

A Golden Shoe! The shoe of a Saint! He stared at her and she seemed to nod, as if to say, 'Yes, take it away. A gift for you.' And then she was wood again. And he, in a dream, fiddle under his arm, golden shoe in his hand, turned and walked to the door. Never again would he be poor.

He stepped outside with a cry of delight – and a heavy hand fell on his shoulder as a cry went out. 'Stop thief! Capital crime! Look! The golden shoe from St Uncumber's Shrine.'

Sobbing and protesting the little fiddler was dragged to St Paul's Cross, the official place for public announcements. There he was hoicked up high for all to see, while his guilt was proclaimed, and the golden shoe was displayed. In no time at all the churchyard of the cathedral was crammed with gawping onlookers.

'It's the three-legged mare for him!' someone sang out with glee; and 100 more joined the refrain: 'Aye! He's for Tyburn Tree!'

> What if you should catch a thief,
> Catch a thief, catch a thief,
> What if you should catch a thief,
> My Fair Lady
> Hanged he'll be at Tyburn Tree,
> Tyburn Tree, Tyburn Tree,
> Hanged he'll be at Tyburn Tree,
> My Fair Lady.

So the fiddler was to be hanged and everyone was well-pleased because hangings were famous fun in those days, a free spectacle for all the family and rich pickings for all the ale, eel and oyster sellers – not to mention the pickpockets, peepshows and pedlars. Besides, he was a good-looking lad, all the better to sigh and cry over and he'd stolen from the Maid of St Paul's, not your average everyday crime at all. But best of all, he was a musician, his fiddle cradled in the crook of his arm, so there were high hopes of getting a last good tune out of him.

So when the day came, the crowd was already calling out choices, as it clustered round the cart of the condemned when it emerged from Newgate. And there was a fight for a glimpse of the lad as they followed it on its way.

First to St Giles in the Fields, where, at the Leper Hospital, all criminals condemned to death were given 'their last refreshing in this life' – the St Giles bowl of ale. (And whether he drank to his own health or not, at least the fiddler did sip something, which all did agree was right and proper, and better than the foolish teetotaller. He wouldn't even touch a drop, and so they hurried him on. And he was hanged the quicker for it – minutes before his pardon came.)

When the drink was done they all went on, some marching much more merrily, though they showed respect with a more solemn step when they heard the bellman from St Stephens toll. 'Good people pray for the soul of these sinners …' it rang for the ones to be hanged. Some did, and some meant to, but soon all forgot in the growing excitement and anticipation. For now they had come to the end of the town, where Tyburn Tree waited and 'the West' began.

But just before the gallows was the place you could stand, and speak whatever was on your mind, before you stepped up to be hanged. And to the procession's enormous pleasure, the young fiddler said 'Nay'. Being a musician, he didn't want to talk, he just wanted to play. And what was more, although he said he would play for them all, he asked if he could so beside the saint's shrine in St Paul's.

The hangman's thoughts could not be heard amongst the crowd's great roars, and the priest's protests were drowned as well in an outburst of applause. The crowd decided it was fair enough, since the lad had stolen her shoe, that reparation – and celebration – should include St Uncumber too. Ignoring the other offenders who were waiting their turns to swing, they bundled the fiddler onto the cart and back to the city again.

The church had never been so full, with people three deep round the walls. But silence fell upon them all when the lad began to play. The sounds he drew out of his fiddle! Low lilting laughter and sweet sobbing sighs; dreams of young maidens and fishmonger's cries; dirges that froze them to stone in their seats; dances that brought the half-dead to their feet; the rafters were ringing; the belfry bats singing; fish skipped from the water; pigs jigged at the slaughter; fathers forgot to care who kissed their daughters …

Only the lad and the saint seemed unmoved. His face, looking up, was like ice, while she, looking down, was just wood.

Hard wood. Not a trace of last time's living face. It was dead, as he would be too, before long. So his hopes and his music came to an end, and the fiddler fell to the ground. And the crowd, forgetting its purpose, pulled out purses and threw money down. The fiddler lay still in a hail of bright coins past caring anymore. Until a gasp of surprise made him open his eyes … to see the saint smile as she threw her last shoe, to land with a gleam in the musician's pile.

Well, you can imagine the flurry and fuss, the relief and the wild celebration … and how the tongues tattled, rumour ran riot and truth turned to wild speculation. But the brave fiddler lad, they all do agree, lived healthy and wealthy and well.

And did he find the right wife too? Only Uncumber can tell.

14

THE INNS OF COURT

The Inns of Court – the very place one might have thought that rules are kept. For in its hallowed walls the laws are studied in great depth. They must be known in every detail and yet explored again to find the perfect match for each new case. But knowledge sometimes leads more to their breach than the observance. Or so it seemed amongst certain students of law there.

Robert Perceval grew up altogether too well-blessed for his own good. Too blue-blooded to be told off by nurses or tutors, too rich to be restrained from spending as he wished, and too good looking to be refused by any woman. Consequently, he knew no limits of any kind, and so indulged himself in excess of every sort. Even though he was studying law at the best Inn of the Court, he had no notion of self-regulation. Things had come to such a pass that people were at last concerned, and pressed him for his own sake to reduce or turn away from his riotous lifestyle. But he would only laugh, or perform some act of crass stupidity, just to show off to his devil-may-care friends. He even persisted in carrying a rapier more than 3ft long, despite the queen's specific orders to the contrary.

One night he was returning to his rooms near the Temple. He was drunk from a party that had lasted day and night, and left a trail of havoc in its wake. He had, at least, the grace to be slinking in quietly, being well past the hour that the gates would have been opened, had he not always 'oiled' his way with tips.

Almost by the archway that led to his stairs, he stumbled and then fell full length. As he scrambled, cursing, back to his feet, he saw a shadow lurking ahead. 'Who is it?' he asked, but there was no reply. He went on, rapier now ready in his hand. Someone was waiting at the stairs, outlined against the light from the lamp by Robert's room. A man in a cloak, but turned away from him; he couldn't see the face at all. 'What the devil are you doing there?' he demanded, but still there was no response. He grew angry then and tried to catch hold of him, but the figure slipped ahead and away up the stairs. Robert ran after, rapier poised, and as the man turned back towards him he struck. His assailant crumpled, stabbed in the chest, the cloak falling back to reveal who he was. And Robert, peering down in the flickering light, was horrified to see his own face looking up. The dead man was himself.

The shock was so great that he fainted on the spot, and when he came round, the figure had gone. It must have been a dream. Yet the fright was such that for a while Robert changed his ways. But little by little, he lapsed again, returning to his old friends and drinking habits, and laughing at the scare he had had.

That winter, the gatekeeper was woken late one night by a terrible drawn out scream. Fearfully he scrambled out of his warm bed, and went to see what it was. It seemed to have come from somewhere near the Temple, where that rascal Robert Perceval had rooms. The gatekeeper almost turned back then, for he'd had enough trouble from that quarter. But duty drove him on. Down the narrow passageways, and round the church, but he saw no one there. Then he noticed the doors to the stairs were open.

Grumbling he went through, and halfway up the stairs he saw a dead body lying on its back. It was Robert Perceval alright, and the cause of his death was clear. The weapon was still stuck in his chest. But it was odd, because it was his own rapier. And there was no sign of anybody else.

15

THE LAMBETH PEDLAR

Where would London have been without the mercers, the merchants, the shopkeepers, the salesmen of the town? And where would they have been without the out-of-town traders, the chapmen, the market stallholders, the pedlars, the hawkers and all? Without that ever-widening web of dealers taking the goods to buyers wherever they may be, buying and selling and buying and selling again? If not for that chain, with a reduction at every link in the status of the seller, and the size of goods exchanged, money would never have gone round, and London would not have grown at all.

It led to other things too, like making maps. The trade radiating out of London travelled along ever-diminishing passageways, like blood distributed over the whole body of the country. From the arterial routes centred on London – the Roman roads, solid and straight, often strengthened with stone – to lesser highways; to bridleways; to byways; to small lanes; to drover's routes; to footpaths; to sheep trails; to rabbit runs; to foot-flattened grass that sprang up again fast. The traders and the drovers held maps in their heads as they walked to and from the market towns and up and down to London each year. One or two scratched them out on slates or bits of parchment. And then an enterprising chapman drew some out and put them on the back of playing cards to be sold. So the trade in road maps began.

Most major London mercers had several chapmen with whom they regularly dealt. The name came from the title 'cheap men' because the smaller parcels of materials they dealt with, in line with the people they were selling them to, were relatively inexpensive.

Chapmen were small fry, but by no means the bottom of the heap. Yet they could always slide down if times were tough. That, no doubt, is what had happened to John Chapman, the peddler of Swaffham, about whom we've heard so much. He was the one who dreamed a dream that he should go to London Bridge, where he would find a fortune. A Swaffham story that shouldn't concern us here, apart from the London end of the tale. For he and his little dog walked all the way, and stood on London Bridge for three days. But apart from saying his prayers to St Thomas in his chapel there, John Chapman spoke to no one, and no one spoke to him. And no fortune was to be seen.

He was just about to go, when a nearby shopkeeper threw his dog a bone. It turned out he had a dog of his own, so he'd noticed John's hanging round hungrily for days. He was a silversmith and doing well. But what was John doing, simply standing and waiting, neither selling nor buying, as far as he could tell? When he heard that they had come there all due to a dream, he laughed and laughed, and told John he was a fool. He himself had had a dream that seemed much the same. He had dreamt of a garden in a place called Swaffham, with a tree, and beneath that a whole pot of gold. Apart from making him smile in his sleep, there was no more good to come out of it. For dreams, he said, were only fancies no one should pursue. But John had heard something that made him smile too, so he thanked the man and took his name. Then he hurried home, where he found that gold in his own back garden, just as foretold in his new friend's dream.

But what happened after, once John Chapman was rich? Well, when he was done with handing out money back home, he got in his fine coach and he rolled up to town. And he went to London Bridge to give thanks to St Thomas, patron saint of London, and to Henry the smith too, for the dream which had made John's dream come true.

Well the silversmith was delighted when heard the good news. But he was a good man, and wealthy enough already, so he wouldn't take a penny by way of thanks from John. But he did agree to go to the George to celebrate. Back there then, towards the end of Queen Bess's glorious reign, it was the finest of taverns, right by the bridge, in Southwark, just as it is to this day.

So they sat down to drink and to dine of the best, and their dogs scrapped for bones beneath the table with the rest. They talked of this and that, and the change in Chapman's fortunes, and how that would make his whole life better from now on.

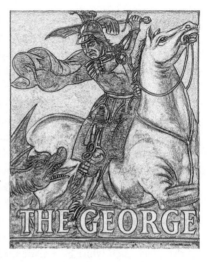

'But no,' said John; though most was an improvement, there were some things he hadn't reckoned on. On his way in his coach, he had come the same route that he had walked before when he was destitute. Last time he'd had to beg a bone or a bite, and a chance to sleep on some straw for the night. It was rough and it was tough, but one thing was clear enough – the way you were treated showed what folks were really like. But now he was rich there was nothing but smiles. Everyone was there to help, new friends gathering like flies. All of a sudden it was hard to tell what was true and what were lies.

Henry Smith couldn't help smiling. John Chapman was such a simple, honest man. At the end of the evening they parted good friends, although they made no arrangement to meet up again.

But next morning, when Henry thought harder, he realised John was not simple at all. For the pedlar had made him consider matters that he'd not thought of before. Henry had always seen kindness in people, but was that because he had never been poor? How generous was he? And what about his friends? How could he know who was truly as charitable as they might pretend?

The question worried him so much that he couldn't work properly, so he went across to St Thomas's chapel for some help.

After the trouble Thomas had had, surely he had some advice on seeing into people's hearts? Henry stayed and prayed, and watched people pass. Men, women, and children too, coming and going with their secrets all hidden inside. And then he realised. He would only discover the truth if he himself were disguised.

His little dog was very pleased when Henry came out to find that instead of stopping at the shop they were going for a walk. When he turned right off the bridge towards Southwark, Bankside, the dog went into the lead, guessing at once where they were going. 'The Stews', as they were called, were the brothels near the prison, where they had been ever since the Bishop of Winchester first licensed the women to work, with dues all paid to him, of course. The women then had to wear little white aprons to show what their trade was, and when they stood outside, waiting for custom in the darkness of the street, their white bibs made them look like geese. So they were known as 'The Bishop's Geese'. But now, of course, the rules were different, and the women waited in the brothel house.

Henry had been going there ever since his wife had died, several years before, in yet another unsuccessful childbirth. So he had neither children nor a wife waiting at home. But he always saw the same woman at the brothel; they were comfortable together and he was fond of her. Today, however, she was in for a surprise – a different service altogether, although he paid the usual fee.

She thought it such a great jape that he should want to disguise himself; she even managed to get another woman to help. And with much laughter and teasing they set to work on him. His neat curled beard had grey wool and dirt twisted into it, to make it look dingy and long. His hair was straggled and knotted with honey and bits of straw, his face and hands stained with walnut juice. Finally, they exchanged his smart cloak, doublet and hose for ragged beggar's clothes, and his fine leather boots for things that seemed more holes than footwear. By the time they were done, he was unrecognisable, and they even put spots on the dog so that she wouldn't give him away either.

However, as they pointed out, he did not want to be taken for a vagrant without proper employment, and be whipped out of town. So they put some bits and pieces in a pack to wear on his back, and gave him a pedlar's pouch too, so he could pass as a hawker of some sort. And they warned him too not to be tempted to talk – that would give him away at once. 'Pretend you cannot speak,' they said, 'that might get you some charity too.' So he learnt the thumb to tongue sign that explained he was dumb.

He had decided, meanwhile, who he was going to test: an alderman on the governing council of Mitcham parish. Henry knew him well, and often gave him money, as he was a noted benefactor to the poor.

It seemed like a game at first. It was a fine afternoon, and pleasant to be outside, and his broken shoes were not as uncomfortable as he had feared. But as he walked along the street, his dog beside him, he was shocked to see how many people moved aside so he didn't come too near to them, and looked annoyed too, as if they had assumed he would have the decency to get himself out of their way first. He soon got the hint and did as was expected, especially when he saw ladies coming. But even then he almost caused offence, for he did it with a sweep of his arm, almost bowing as any gentleman would, and so appeared to be making fun of them. Even eye contact seemed unseemly from a poor pedlar, such as he was pretending to be. There was a lot to learn of this other world.

At last he got to Mitcham and he quickened his pace as he neared his friend's house. He almost gave himself away by going to the front door, but just in time he remembered to walk round the back. Unfortunately, his little dog didn't understand that. She had been there quite often as a welcome visitor, even allowed into the library with her master. So she barked and whined and scratched at the kitchen door until it was flung open by a furious servant who promptly emptied a pot of slops all over the poor creature. 'The next one is for you,' she said to Henry. 'If you don't get your filthy face out this instant.'

Mindful of the good advice he'd been given, he didn't protest out loud, but pointed into his mouth and shook his head. Then he took off his pack and made a dumb show of having things to sell and being very hungry too.

Meanwhile, however, his poor dog, who had never been treated so badly in its life, began to run round barking hysterically.

The master of the house himself came out to see what was going on, and Henry was hard put not to call out to his friend. But this time he saw the alderman in an altogether different light. Gone were his gentle charitable ways! Despite the pitiful show, Henry put on, he had his footman out in a moment, and Henry and dog were kicked round the house and out of the gates. What was worse, he wasn't even allowed to gather up his pack again, and all his goods, were left behind. If Henry had indeed been trying to make a living as a pedlar, that single thoughtless uncharitable act would have ruined him.

He was glad to get back to his own clothes, and his own life. But he couldn't forget the experience he'd had. It had taught him so much. Over the next few months he went out as a poor man again and again, and now he saw the generosity of some people too. Sometimes they were people that he knew, and he was delighted to find them as kind as they had always seemed. But more often than not, it was people along the way, a few barely better off than beggars themselves, who would give him a drink, or a piece of bread, or simply treat him as if he also was a human being worthy of the name. In the back of his mind he always hoped to meet with John Chapman again, and to say 'this time it is I who should thank you, for telling me what you knew.'

Little by little, as the years went by, Henry Smith was more often a penniless pedlar than a rich silversmith. Mostly he was on the south side of the river, spreading out from London into Surrey and Kent. From parish to parish he went, testing the true nature of the people he met. In time he became so well known, with his little dog always at his side, that he gained a new name, 'Dog Smith'.

One place where he felt welcome, more often than not, was Lambeth, a new but fast-growing parish on the south bank of the river, surrounded by fields and farms. Perhaps it was because it was not a rich area, that the people seemed more generous there. Often Henry would stop in what became his favourite spot, the churchyard of St Mary's church. It had a particularly sunny seat, which no one ever objected to him occupying for a while. In the end, the parishioners got so used to seeing the old man resting there, with his faithful friend lying at his feet, that they put out a little wooden bowl full of water for the dog to drink. By now the poor creature was old and getting feeble, but she always found the strength to wag her tail in thanks for any little kindnesses. Henry felt he'd lost part of himself when she eventually died.

Soon after that, the rector of St Mary's church, to his great surprise, had a visit from Henry Smith, renowned benefactor and wealthy silversmith. For some reason that he could not fathom, Mr Smith offered a considerable sum of money for an old pedlar's dog to be buried in the churchyard. It was the sort of sum that could not be refused. The worthy gentleman also paid for a fine stained-glass window for the church, depicting, of all things, old Dog Smith himself with the little creature in question. But, as Henry explained, it was not the first time a pedlar should be represented in so grand a way. For in Swaffham, a pedlar called John Chapman had come into a great sum of money, and had paid for a whole new church – with effigies of himself in it. And his dog! The rector had heard of the generous John Chapman, but could hardly imagine so respectable a gentleman could ever have been a poor pedlar. But as Henry said, blessed are the poor and meek … and the window he gave the church was a treasure indeed.

After the loss of his dog, Henry was more often in his poor clothes than as himself. In this guise he returned once more to Mitcham, and this time the alderman had him caught and whipped as a vagrant, to teach him a lesson he would never forget.

He did not forget it either. When the time came for him to die, his will was a surprise to everyone. His large estate and other assets were divided up between those parishes and people who had shown him true charity. Lambeth in particular did very well, and St Mary's church was bequeathed an osier ground, later enclosed as a meadow, called Pedlar's Acre.

But Mitcham got nothing at all – to the surprise and disappointment of the alderman, who had always cultivated Henry Smith as a personal friend.

16

REBECCA
AND THE RING

Well it wasn't in my time, nor was it in yours. It was the time when rivers ran their own course. The Thames slipped by as stately easy as you please, then raced full fierce and fast, and once past London town, the River Lea came pouring down to feed it from the north-east side. Both rivers ebbed and flowed with the tide, the Lea so powerfully that tidal mills along its banks ground corn both day and night.

Queen Matilda, Henry I's wife, had reason to respect its might. On her way to Barking Abbey she tried to ford the river at 'Brembel Lega', the 'bramble meadow land' that gave its name to Bromley. Her pious purpose paramount, she forced her horse on, failing to feel the full pull of the current until it dragged her down. She almost drowned. Restored to solid ground at last, she asked for a bridge or 'bow' to be built. So the area became 'Bromley by Bow', and prospered accordingly, for there were few places at that time where people could safely dance as the new song asked, 'Over my Lady Lea.'

Hackney Wick was just a kink in the bank, a place where small boats could harbour. Stepney was Stebenhythe, a simple landing place. There were no barriers to hold the river back, or drainage ditches and diversions to claim the land from the water. To the east of London, all was mostly marsh, the rivers winding through, with various flooding branches. A damp home for fishermen and eel catchers, and a haven for wildfowl and all who fed on them; although hunters carefully picked their way for fear of finding a watery grave.

But little by little, London townsmen were turning their eyes towards it. Bishops of London owned the Manor of Stepney, and one, Dunstan, on becoming a saint had his name added to the church there. Edward I improved the banks, and made Stepney a place for a parliament, and Mayors of London, encouraged by this, promptly acquired estates. It was land where they could expand, and perhaps enjoy a bit of sport, within the easy reach of court. If they wanted more, they could follow the marsh north, and meet with Epping Forest royal hunting grounds. So – as in those days a moment caught in the regal gaze could raise one from the depths to the heights of praise – a Stepney Marsh mudbank, just an 'ey' in the ooze, gained name and fame as the 'Isle of Dogs' where a royal pack could kennel. And then James I came to the throne, and wanting the fresh air, clear of the Plague zone, and the chance to hunt ever nearer to home, he built his hunting lodge and palace at Bromley by Bow.

So, everyone who was anyone was soon seen on the Stepney flatlands. And one who was definitely someone – in his own eyes at least – was the noble Sir Berry. He was out hunting with a party of friends, celebrating the christening of his son and heir. Full of the joys of life, and the happy assurance of a stable future, he gave his horse its head, chasing after a hound that had got the scent of something more than fowl. Not noticing how far back his friends had fallen, nor how late the day had become, he was caught suddenly in a thick marsh mist that rose out of nowhere. It was so clammy and confusing, even the dog was utterly confounded and crept back whining at the echo of its bark.

Sir Berry reined in and turned back to join the others, but it was impossible to retrace his steps. Hour after hour, he wandered in circles, until the horse stopped abruptly and refused to take another step. Then he heard a sound from behind that at first he took to be a hunting horn. When it came again he realised it was the wail of a child. He turned the horse and headed back towards it, and now the beast went on without objection. At last they came to a flickering light which turned out to be a candle in the window of a ramshackle house, hardly more than a reed hut. The dog was already at the door and he pushed in after. Inside a fire was roaring, with a woman sitting by it. She turned as he entered.

'Thank God,' he said, 'I thought I was lost.'

'Thank Lady Luck too,' she answered. 'It was her wheel who brought you here.'

He was taken aback, both by her words and the way she spoke, so directly, without deference. 'I am no gambler, guided by luck,' he said curtly. 'In these settled times I can decide my own path.'

'I wouldn't be so sure of that,' she replied. 'But come, sit by the fire. There is little enough to eat, but you're welcome to all I have. Or perhaps you would like to see to your horse first. Tell me, does he have a white blaze between his ears?' She smiled at his astonishment. 'Ah, then you are the man I was expecting. As fate foretold. And if you want your proof of fortune's power, retrace your steps tomorrow in the light, and see the place your horse had stopped before you heard my daughter cry.' It was only then that he saw a baby, cradled in her arms. A tiny creature younger than his son, but with eyes of the most astonishing blue.

'Hold her, if you will,' the woman said, 'while I find you some food. And let you get to know her too, for tomorrow I will be gone, and she must go with you. Forgive me, but she will repay the task of looking after her. Rebecca is her name, and she is destined for good fortune and fame. As I was told, and swear it's true, her fate is to marry into the noble family of Berry. So whoever you are, sir, she will well look after you.'

Shocked into silence, Sir Berry held the child, ate the food given him, and waited for the first light of morning to escape. As soon as he could see he crept outside, got onto his horse, and for want of other options, retraced his steps. Soon enough, he came to where the horse had halted so determinedly. Another step, he could see now, would have landed them both in the water, the River Lea still running so high and wild they would not have stood a chance.

The dog was whining and running backwards and forwards in the direction of the house. Again Sir Berry could hear the child crying. But this time, as he stepped inside, the woman said nothing. She sat in the chair, cold and dead. The prophecy still running in his head, Sir Berry picked up the child, wrapped her in soft well-woven cloth, and carried her back to the river. 'This child to marry into my house? This girl to wed my son? This nobody?' He could not let it be. 'Her fate ends here!' he cried, and threw her into the angry water. Then in the early morning sun he made his way back home.

The river wound its way down towards a mill. The cloth was tightly woven, the girl held buoyant. Above the mill race, a fisherman had set his net and was already there to see what the night had brought. To his astonishment, he saw a child spinning in the stream and quickly fished her out. He and his wife had no children of their own, and they were delighted at the river's gift. Embroidered carefully in the corner of the cloth was the letter 'R'. When the parson told them what it said, they called her the first name that came into their head – Rebecca. The river's daughter.

Time passed, and Sir Berry's son, John, grew into a fine youth with his father's love of hunting. One day, while riding by the Lea, he felt thirsty, and seeing a cluster of fishermen's huts he stopped to ask for a drink. An old man called for his daughter to bring out a jug of small beer, but the moment John looked into her blue eyes he forgot his thirst and everything else. They talked a little together and the more he heard her speak the more he wondered how she could be a simple fisherman's daughter.

'Ah, but Sir!' her foster father explained proudly. 'She is the daughter of the Lea, she is. She came with her name embroidered on fine cloth and no matter what we teach her she can never learn enough. She can sew and spin and do anything. Next thing she'll be reading and writing!'

The lad was so love-struck, he couldn't keep his mouth shut, and word of this girl soon reached his father. What he heard made him so concerned that he got on his horse and went straight to the girl's house. One look at her and he knew right enough, and his fears were confirmed by the cloth. As he listened to her father, his thoughts were whirling, but soon he saw what line to take.

'It seems that she is destined for a higher life,' he said. 'Would you like her to read and write? If you trust her to me, I will do what is right.'

The fisherman and his wife were broken-hearted to let their daughter go. But they did not want to stand in her way. And so, for the second time, Sir Berry took Rebecca on his horse before him and rode away.

Taking her to a dressmaker he had her fitted out with cloaks and gowns and all she might need for a long journey, as if he was indeed the second father to her that he had promised to be. Meanwhile he wrote to his cousin in the North country.

> This beautiful girl is going to destroy both my son and myself.
> Guard her carefully and as soon as you may have her killed for John's sake
> with this ring of mine I send proof I am
> your loving cousin
> Sir J. Berry

Then, giving Rebecca the sealed letter to deliver for him, Sir Berry hired a coach and coachmen to take her to his cousin, and sent her off to certain death.

The journey to the North was long, the roads were rough, and times had changed since the promise of peace and stability brought by James. Charles was on the throne now, and there were open arguments between the King and City guilds, and Parliament too. While the king's men were occupied, keeping an eye on the south, the King's Highway was left to look after itself. Highwaymen and brigands were quick to take control of roads; cutpurses and thieves closed in on coaching inns. One night Rebecca's bags were rifled while she slept, though the looters found nothing but the letter from Sir Berry, with the ring tied round it. The seal looked important, so they broke it open, and their leader, who had learnt his letters, read it out loud.

But when they heard what it said, and they saw how sweet she looked, they were all so indignant that they made a scribe revise it, and carefully wash a few letters away.

> This beautiful girl is going to bring joy to my son and myself. Guard her carefully and as soon as you may have her married to John with this ring of mine.
> your loving cousin
> Sir J. Berry

So when at last Rebecca arrived, and delivered the letter and ring to Sir Berry's cousin and his wife, she was welcomed with open arms, and soon made to feel part of the family.

Meanwhile, young John Berry had joined King Charles' cavalry. As the civil strife worsened he was sent here and there, to gather or give support as needed. Finding himself not far from his father's cousins, he decided to pay them a visit. What was his delight to find Rebecca staying there, and then to his amazement he was shown his father's letter. He wrote at once to thank him, and to make sure that he would be coming to the wedding, preparations for which were begun at once.

Trouble on the roads made communications bad, and Sir Berry did not receive the letter for some time. When he did, he could not understand how things could have gone so awry, but, hoping to prevent the worst from happening, he called for his coach and four, ordering his coachman to drive him with all haste to the North.

The journey passed this time without trouble on the road, but Sir Berry was too late. The church bells were ringing, the floor was strewn with flowers, and the ring was already on the finger of the bride when he arrived. But even when his cousin – waving the fateful letter – congratulated him on finding a daughter who'd 'bring as much joy' as Rebecca, John's angry father refused to accept that the deed was done. Pushing past well-wishers, he caught hold of the bride and, taking her to his coach, he bundled her inside. 'I regret to tell you,' he said, 'but your mother has died.' Then he called to the coachman to turn about, and return to London again.

Rebecca sat in silent shock, huddled in her cloak, almost all she'd had time to snatch as she was hurried out. The journey took fewer days, for they only stopped to allow the horses to be changed. And the coachman too, when he got so tired he fell asleep and slipped off his seat. But all the way Sir Berry sat glaring, refusing to explain.

So, at last, they arrived at London town, but instead of turning eastwards they drove on south, heading for London Bridge. The morning was just dawning when the coach finally stopped. Sir Berry got down and, helping her out, he led Rebecca onto the bridge. Past the stalls and houses, where hardly a soul was stirring, to the gap where they could see directly down on to the river. The tide was turning and the Thames was high, a seething mass of black murderous water swirling swiftly by.

'Why are we here?' Rebecca asked. 'What has this to do with my mother?' When Sir Berry didn't answer, she looked up into his face, and the rage she saw in his eyes made her suddenly afraid.

'Your mother died many years ago,' he said, 'when you were born. She told me you must marry my son. She was wrong. You will never be his wife. Give me back my ring that you stole from me, through him!'

She bowed her head, and slipped it slowly from her finger, holding it warm for a moment before she handed it over. 'Take back your ring,' she said, 'but you can never break the love I have with John.'

He pulled her closer to the river's edge. Holding the ring high, he flung it far out into the water, and they both watched it sink. 'Now I do swear,' Sir Berry cried, 'that if I ever see your hand once more, without that wedding ring upon it, I will throw you too into the Thames, as tide is high again.' And then he was gone, Rebecca left alone.

She did not go home. She felt she could not let her foster parents know – after all they had done and hoped for – how badly things had gone wrong. But her feet led her eastwards, knowing no other way to go, and she followed the river aimlessly along the north side. Passing Billingsgate, and the fish market as it was beginning to stir, she came at last to a tavern overlooking the Isle of Dogs, and there she stopped and rested in the shelter of the door.

Little did she guess it was a smugglers' meeting place. 'The Devil's Tavern', it was called by all around. An inn where people 'watched the wall' and did not look at who came past, and asked no questions about what was rolled in barrels, in or out. But where else could a young girl in a bridal dress, with only a cloak and a handful of coins, hope to hide with no one to pry? There were private rooms aplenty where she could stay if she could pay. And when her money ran out, she asked if there was work. The cook, whose heart was as warm as the fine French brandy that the tavern somehow always had in plentiful supply, gave her a chance as a kitchen maid.

The tavern keeper was well repaid, however, for taking her on, for despite her looks they soon found that she worked as fast as any seasoned fish wife, not only cutting, gutting and cleaning fish, but also cooking it, and other dishes too. She could make good solid meals to satisfy a working man, and yet she also knew, from her time in the North, how to create the most delicate titbit, to please the palate of the highest gentle born. It soon became a fashion, even for the royal court, to stop at the tavern and feast away their cares.

Meanwhile, John had followed his father back to London as quickly as he could, wondering what had happened to his bride. What was his horror to hear from his father that Rebecca had slipped into the river and died. On her way to her sick mother, Sir Berry explained, she had tried to ford the Lea when the tide was too high. John was inconsolable. He couldn't sleep, and wouldn't eat. He almost lost all will for life. But as the time passed, civil war broke out in earnest. Now there was nothing for him to do but fight.

Years passed. Then one day Rebecca was asked by the cook to go to Billingsgate market and pick out the best from the fresh catches there, for she was to help prepare a feast for some very important guests. Returning loaded with the finest fish to be found, Rebecca began to cut and gut the biggest one of the batch. In its stomach something was shining. It was a ring. A wedding ring. And as she pulled it out, she saw it was her own. Slowly she slipped it onto her finger and for a moment stood there motionless, savouring the feel of it there, back where it belonged.

Then she got on with her task, preparing the fish dish for the feast. It was a wedding party, she heard now, so she decorated the plate with flowers. That evening, her work done, she heard the guests arrive, and peeped out as they went past to see what they looked like. First to come was a white-haired man, with his back to her, talking to someone. But then he turned, and she saw to her shock that he was old Sir Berry. And the man he was talking to – oh! He looked thin and gaunt, to her loving eyes, and one cheek was scared with a long thin line. But yet he was still her John. 'He's the one getting married,' said the cook, who'd also come for a quick look. 'He doesn't look happy though, does he?' And indeed he seemed as sad and pale as if he was at his own funeral.

Rebecca went and washed her face, and did the best she could with her dress. The wedding guests were seated now, and waiting for the feast. Picking up the great fish dish that she'd prepared so carefully, Rebecca walked into the room with her head held high. Even in her serving clothes, she was beautiful. But that was not what caught the bridegroom's eye. It was something to do with the way she moved. He gave a start; he felt his whole heart jump. Then she looked straight into his face and he was sure. Her blue, blue eyes held his against all possibilities. It could not be, and yet he knew it was.

Sir Berry saw his son leaping to his feet, and, looking at Rebecca, he recognised her too. He opened his mouth to speak, but she stopped in front of him, and putting down the fish, she held up her left hand. 'I have something to show you,' she said, and pointed to the ring. Her wedding ring. His signet ring.

And in that moment at long last, Sir Berry knew that he was beaten. 'What fate has set down,' he said, 'I see now cannot be undone. Here is Rebecca, my son's true bride. What God has joined together, we cannot then divide.'

And John? He was still staring. Hoping, yet afraid that he could not believe his eyes. 'I thought you were lost,' he said to her. 'They told me you were drowned.'

Rebecca laughed, and took his hand. 'My love, I am a child of the water. The river would never let me down.'

The monument of Dame Rebecca Berry, widow of Sir John, is at St Dunstan and All Saints church, Stepney. It is in the shape of a shield, with a coat of arms above, which shows three fish, and what appears to be a ring. Below is an inscription:

As fair a mind
As e'er yet lodg'd in womankind.
So she was dress'd whose humble life
Was free from pride, was free from strife.
Still the same humble she appears
The same in youth, the same in years,
The same in low and high estate.

17

LIGHT-HEARTED
HIGHWAYMAN

Stephen Bunce was a real gentleman of the road. It was almost a pleasure to have to deliver your purse to him; he robbed with such politeness and lightness of touch. And he was so quick thinking and witty too. He nearly made you laugh at your own sad plight. And he certainly had everyone else laughing when they heard about the tricks he played.

But like anyone, he had his ups and downs of course. Sometimes he was in pocket and riding high, and sometimes he had to walk the length and breadth of Epping Forest on foot. Once he was doing that with a friend. Maybe she was a lady friend and he had started out with other things on his mind. But there in front of them was an old man walking slow and steady along the path, leading a donkey on a longish rope behind him. Too good an opportunity to miss.

Stephen winked at his friend, and they both crept up close, as quiet as could be. Then Stephen carefully slipped the halter off the donkey, and fitted it on to his own head, falling straight into the same easy ambling way of walking as the donkey. Meanwhile, his friend took the animal and slipped away through the trees with it, going to the market by a roundabout route.

Stephen kept going until they were safely away, and then he stumbled slightly, jerking on the rope. The old man looked round, and nearly fell over backwards in surprise when he saw that instead of a donkey he was leading a man.

'What on earth are you doing there?' he asked.

'Oh master,' sighed Stephen, on an almost braying mournful note. 'You don't want to know. It's too bad to tell.'

By now, of course, the old man was beside himself with curiosity. 'I insist on an explanation,' he said.

'Then we'd better sit down,' said Stephen. 'For it is a sorry tale indeed.' He settled himself with a sigh, leaning back against a tree, and after a moment, the old man followed suit. 'It's like this,' Stephen went on in a confessional whisper. 'You see, I was a man too, before. But not a very good one. In fact, a very bad one indeed. I committed a sin. So bad I was punished. Just like that! I was turned into a donkey.'

'A donkey?'

'Yes. As you saw for yourself.'

By now the old man could hardly believe his ears. But it was true, he had seen the donkey. In fact, he had been making it work all year long. 'What sin was it?' he asked, all agog.

'I don't like to say,' said Stephen hanging his head.

'But you must! I might need to know myself!'

So Stephen leant slowly forward and whispered something into the old man's ear. What exactly it was, nobody knows, for no one else was there to hear. But the old man's eyes went as round as a silver shilling. 'You poor, poor fellow,' he said. 'Well take that halter off your head. You have certainly been punished enough. Just make sure you don't do it again.'

'I blame the drink. I'd had too much,' admitted Stephen shamefacedly. 'But now you've given me a second chance, I swear I'll never touch a drop again.'

The two men parted like good friends, and went their separate ways. The old man returned home with nothing in his pocket; Stephen went to share out the money from the donkey. He didn't make very much. It wasn't a particularly good beast. The man who bought it sold it on almost at once.

Meanwhile, the old man needed a replacement. It took a good few months before he scraped up enough to be able to go back to the market. But what was his astonishment on his arrival there, to see his same old donkey standing waiting to be sold. 'Drink again, I bet,' said the old man sadly. 'Well, you know where that leads. It's no use expecting me to help you out again.' And off he went to find himself a better behaved beast.

Stephen Bunce, he was a fast one. No stopping him. Although, sometimes he found walking slowly led to quicker money. Another time, he was strolling through the forest when he heard the sound of horse's hooves on the road nearby. Climbing up a tree, he could see it was a gentleman, riding an extremely fine horse. He flung himself down on the side of the road, pressing his ear to the grass.

The gentleman naturally stopped when he saw someone lying like that. 'Are you all right?' he asked.

'Shush,' said Stephen. 'I'm listening.'

'Listening to what?' asked the other in surprise.

'The fairies of course!' whispered Stephen. 'Such beautiful music isn't it?'

'But I can't hear anything,' the gentleman said.

'Oh dear,' said Stephen. 'You don't want to miss this. I'll tell you what, this must be an especially good listening spot. You can have a turn here for a minute, just so you get a bit of it.'

'But my horse is a bit lively,' said the man. 'I don't want it to run off.'

'Oh, for goodness sake!' exclaimed Stephen, pretending to be getting annoyed. 'I suppose I'll have to hold it for you then. But hurry up.' So he got up and the man got down, quick as you can. He lay down on the ground, while Stephen took his horse.

'Press your ear right down,' he said as he climbed on the horse's back. 'Can you hear anything now?' But all the man could hear was his horse's hooves on the road, as Stephen galloped away laughing.

He was a merry man all the way through. Right until he climbed his very last tree. The one that all highwaymen, however witty and tricky they were, expected to meet with in the end: Tyburn tree. Only one way down.

18

LODGER OF SOHO SQUARE

When Soho Square was new, it was a much grander affair altogether, laid out with tall elegant trees, and beautiful flowers and a playful fountain. In the middle of the sparkling water was a splendid statue. It was meant to be the perfect place to take your ease, which, of course, it was. For it was all done in honour of the restored monarch Charles II, and the statue was of his royal self. And no one could have known better than him what pleasure it was to be able to sit back and relax, surrounded by ladies and other such beauties, in the centre of your own capital city. The statue is still there, restored to almost its original position, if not its original graceful state. For much has changed, not least the square's name. Back in those days it was called King Square. And a sought-after spot it certainly was, with high-priced houses all round. Even after the merry monarch had gone, and the new century had begun.

At that time, there was a house in the square that was too big for the current master. He and his wife lived in the main part of it, and the rest was let as furnished lodgings. A wealthy gentleman had recently taken up occupation. A charming man, but rather retiring, only desiring to keep himself to himself. 'The perfect lodger, in fact,' as the mistress remarked.

The servants, especially the maids, were also relieved. The mistress liked everything to be 'just so', which meant there was always plenty for them to do, without having anyone else traipsing in and out, or leaving dirty marks on the carpets. At that time the list of servant's tasks was daunting, and the lower you were in the pecking order, the longer it was. For the 'maid of all work', who was right at the bottom, it seemed endless. She was only thirteen, and

new too, and already wishing she could go back home. She'd get up in the dark, haul water for baths, clean the grate, lay and light the fires, sweep and dust, wash and scrub and even mend clothes, empty the chamber pots, make the beds, help in the kitchen as required, and sometimes run out to the shops. By the time she was finished it was dark again, and she was ready to drop.

One day the butler called her, and gave her a letter to be taken to the lodger. It had been delivered to the front door, and it seemed to be rather important. Later she glimpsed the gentleman himself, looking rather pale, on his way to talk to the master and mistress. Word soon seeped out downstairs. It seemed his brother had died; it was all very sudden and sad. And now there was a lot to arrange. The coffin would have to be taken to the family vault, which was a day's journey away. So the lodger had asked if it might stay in the house overnight, and they would go on the next day.

Of course the master said yes. The poor gentleman was obviously in such distress. But it didn't seem right to have the corpse carried to his rooms upstairs. Then the mistress had an idea. There was space for the coffin to be laid in the library, which wouldn't be needed that evening.

So that was arranged, but the coffin bearers didn't arrive until well after supper. It was a bit of a nasty night, which had delayed them, apparently. Although the mistress had stayed up to see the coffin brought in, and taken to the library, and the coffin bearers ushered out all politely, it was up to the servants after that, of course, to clean up that bit of mud they'd brought in from outside and to make sure all doors were locked fast, and the lights put out. And naturally, the poor maid of all work still had to do the final tasks, damping down the fire in the kitchen and so on.

Actually she was quite glad of a bit of time on her own in the warm and the firelight because she thought it was a bit ghoulish to have a coffin in the house like that. It'd be different if there was a wake, and people sitting round it, but not sitting in there on its own.

She must have sat down herself for a moment, and dozed off, for all of a sudden she was woken by the sound of the kitchen door creaking open. Looking up, still half-asleep, she thought at first she was dreaming. In through the door glided a terrifying apparition. Tall, deathly pale, wrapped in a shroud – it was the corpse itself out of the coffin and walking. Too shocked even to scream, she managed to dodge around it and race upstairs to the master and mistress' bedroom. She was that upset she didn't wait to knock – she just burst straight in.

As you might imagine they woke in a state of confusion, and hastily lit candles to see what was going on. But once they had, there was no need for the girl to try to explain, for the awful corpse had followed after her. There it stood, blocking their exit, grinning and grimacing in such a menacing fashion that the mistress had the vapours, and the master, brave though he was, didn't dare to move an inch.

Then suddenly, the whole house seemed caught up in the nightmare, with odd noises and clatter and confusion, as if an army of the dead was storming through. The servants in the attic tried to come down, but the door was mysteriously locked, so they started hammering and shouting, to add to the mayhem. The master attempted to get up then, but the corpse pointed a finger at him, and he collapsed in terror, while the maid and the mistress dived under the bed.

Eventually they realised the noises had stopped. The girl emerged from under the bed, and saw that the ghoul in the doorway had gone. But when they all went out to look, they saw a number of other things had gone too. Silverware and gold ornaments, some fine ivories, and all sorts of other valuables. Precious pictures had been pulled off the walls, the master's portmanteau rifled, and drawers emptied out all over the floor. The coffin was empty too, of course. So was the lodger's bedroom.

It seemed that the spectre and corpse had in fact been very much alive, and was the theatrical half of a duo of thieves. His counterpart was rather more private, the quiet brains behind the scheme. And a perfect gentleman lodger.

19

BECKY OF BEDLAM

There was a merchant in Fish Street Hill, by London Bridge. He had several servants, amongst them a young maid who was pretty enough and worked hard, too – although if you didn't do that you would soon be out on your ear. But she was a bit of an innocent, easily impressed by the things she didn't know about, and there were plenty of those! Her name was Rebecca, quickly reduced to 'Becky'. She was certainly at everybody's beck and call.

The merchant took in lodgers, and one of them was a student. One of Becky's many jobs was to clean his room. Oh, how she loved that job! She would save it till last, so she could look forward to it all day. For he had many books, and since she could neither read nor write, to her they were things of great mystery and strange beauty. She loved to touch them, and once, greatly daring, she opened one, and ran her fingers along the letters, pretending she could read. She liked to imagine what they were about, making up stories in her head to fit. Being rather a dreamer, she sometimes got lost in her ideas and spent far longer in his room than she realised, which was why one day she got caught. She actually had the book in her hand when she heard the door opening behind her, so there was no denying it. She was so scared she started to cry, thinking she would lose her place because of it, and then what would she do?

But he was more than kind. He said he was glad she liked his books, and even offered to show her them one day. When he heard that she couldn't read, he patted her on the shoulder, and smiled. 'Maybe I will have to teach you,' he said.

And so they began to meet. Just for a few minutes at first, but it soon got longer. And he soon got interested in teaching her other things. More entertaining for him than books. Once she got to know him, she realised that he was younger than she thought, not all that much older than her, and not that bad looking either. And he was so kind to her. Nobody had ever taken an interest in her before, not like that. She knew it was wrong, but she liked to please him in return, and before the year was out, she was wildly in love with him. And he her, she was sure of that. The way he kissed her! So it led on, naturally enough, and he got her to slip into his room at night. She was a bit afraid something would come of it, but then even if it did, maybe it was a bit early to start a family but they would manage, she was sure. Plenty of people did. When he talked about what he would do after he finished his studies, she saw herself in his plans. Little Becky the wife of a learned man – whoever would have believed it!

And then the time came when he had to take his exams, and of course there were no moments free for Becky then. But she understood. It was all for her good too.

And then they were done. And then she heard from the cook that he was going to move on. And she was hugging her secret to herself, waiting for him to ask – she was ready to go. And then he was packing and the boxes going downstairs and no one else looking for a moment. And he came up to her with a smile on his face, and she smiled back. Oh she was so happy! And he reached out and caught hold of her hand – the left one, the wedding hand – he opened it up and kissed it. And then put a gold sovereign right on her palm, and turned away.

She just stood there, staring. She couldn't believe her eyes. The gold so cold on her warm skin. And then she began to scream.

They said she'd had some kind of a fit. And she'd fallen so hard on the ground it must have hurt something, for after that the blood came pouring out, and her skirts all soaked, and she thought she was dying. And it might have been better if she had, cook said. Because there was all the fuss and the disgrace, and of course she lost her place. Not that she'd have been able to go on doing the work she'd done, even if she still had any sense. Because whatever it was in her left hand she wouldn't let it go, she held it so, and cook almost got bitten when she tried to pry it free. She was out of her wits altogether, that girl.

Nothing the master could do, even if he'd wanted to. No use throwing good money after bad. The only place that would take her in was Bedlam. She was lucky not to be just left in the street. Not that she showed any proper gratitude.

Bedlam had moved to Moorfields by then and it was as nice as pie now for the lunatics. Didn't hardly get chained up at all, and they weren't all together in one big hall. Mind you, that was more for the sake of the warders – it would drive you mad yourself, to be in the same space with all the bellowing and roaring and screaming. Like Hell. That's one reason it got the name Bedlam. St Mary of Bethlehem, it had been in the beginning, when it was a priory, but that was hundreds of years before – no one remembered that any more. But the place it was at now, at Moorfields, well that was like a holiday. Far more than they deserved, most people with any sense said. They had different 'wards', as they called them now; one was for 'Curables' that they thought the doctors could cure – doctors, yes! They had them and all! 'Talk about lucky!' people said.

But when they got Becky there, she was wild as a cat. Screamed and fought and all sorts. It took two men to force her hand open, and get that sovereign out. And afterwards she kept on searching and searching, trying to find it, in her hand, up her skirts, in a crack on the floor that was much too small, you name it, she looked there – it was laughable.

But after a few months she began to look like she'd managed to lose herself too. Eyes all empty, not even seeming to hear, just sitting there, rocking, rocking, rocking. That's when they moved her on, into the incurables. She wasn't any bother then, at least. You could forget her altogether until something sparked her off. No one ever worked out what it was, maybe a sound that got through, or a movement, but it would switch her on again, like a wind-up toy. And she'd do all that searching stuff again. Or sometimes cry and tear her hair. Only for a bit, but it was enough to satisfy spectators.

For this was the time of George III, when even royalty were mad. It was almost a fashion. And it was certainly fashionable entertainment to go and have a peep at Bedlam. For a penny you could peer into every cell, and see what the lunatics got up to. It was a real laugh sometimes.

And the first Tuesday of every month it was free. Mind you, it was packed, hundreds there, you could hardly move. What you'd do, if you knew the ropes, was to shuffle through with everyone else in a long queue, but when you got to the cell that you liked best, you'd step out of line and hang on the window bars as tight as you could, face pressed against them. Then everybody else just had to go on past.

Becky didn't get many of those dedicated visitors, because most of the time she wasn't doing anything. But you might strike lucky, and get one of those moments worth watching. Besides, you didn't have to fight so hard for the window spot.

Perhaps it wasn't a Tuesday when he came. At any rate it wasn't so full that he couldn't get through. He didn't know she was there, of course. And he wasn't there just to stare, either. Or at least that's what he told himself, although there was an awful fascination in seeing them, one after another. But it was his job now, in a way, to see how people behaved. All that endless studying and those terrifying examinations he thought he'd never pass. But he had, and now he knew that it had all been worth it, because it had led in into a branch of medicine that was quite fascinating. And potentially a promising career too, although he was only a lowly assistant so far. But he was ambitious. Which was why he was here, on a rare day off, to learn whatever he could. If only the large woman in front would hurry up and move along. She was almost blocking the whole corridor, and certainly monopolising the window to the next cell. He was about to push on past, and get ahead at least, but something made him glance through the little gap between the woman's fat shoulder and her hat.

Inside there was a young female, sitting on the floor, facing sideways to the door. With her right finger she was tracing lines on the ground, as if she was reading something in the dust. The fat woman laughed, and the inmate looked up. Her eyes met his, and in that moment of shock, before he could stop himself, her name was on his lips. 'Becky!'

She froze. For an instant he thought he saw a spark of recognition; then she turned away. 'What did you say?' the fat woman asked curiously. 'Is that her name?'

'I ... No ... She just reminded me of someone, that's all,' he said. 'I've no idea who she really is.'

'They call her The Sovereign,' the woman said, with a laugh. 'Funny that – I don't mean the King. It was a gold sovereign, they say. She fought like mad to stop them taking it away. A lover's gift they reckon it was. Or maybe a tip, once he'd done with her. Nobody really knows.'

Becky was still quite young when she died. Perhaps it was her only means of escape. And yet her ghost stayed; they say it is seen to this day. Has she been held there by her sad search for the sovereign? Surely then she would have stayed in Moorfields.

Instead, she followed Bedlam out of the city, first to new premises in St Georges Fields in Southwark, and then later when it moved again, into the countryside near Beckenham. By then, the old name 'Bedlam' had been dropped, and the old ways were also changed for good as knowledge grew, and sympathy too, for illness and trauma hidden inside the mind. In the sunshine and fresh air, surrounded by true care, it was felt that people had a better chance to reshape their lives.

Perhaps Becky's spirit felt this too. And maybe there, at last, long after she died, she found the love and peace that she was due.

20

LUCKY SWEEP

Mrs Montague was one of those ladies envied by her whole circle of acquaintances. She seemed to have everything one could require in life: a wealthy and pleasant husband, a delightful little boy, a splendid house on the corner of Portman Square, and the health and leisure to enjoy it all. And she did, for she was one of those rare but welcome creatures who fully appreciated good fortune.

Her little son was almost five years old, and a dear little thing, although full of high spirits and boyish energy. Luckily he had a nurse who was well used to dealing with children, and seemed the ideal choice for the position. Unfortunately, she had one or two failings, which she kept well hidden. The first was a most unsuitable man friend, who she would meet when out, but who had, of course, never been to the house. The second, possibly even worse, was an occasional taste for the bottle.

That winter was particularly severe, and the Thames had entirely frozen over, and there was tremendous excitement about the Frost Fair on the ice. There were all sorts of fairground booths, and roundabouts, and games, but the highlight was an elephant that was being led across the river just below Blackfriars Bridge. The Montagues' little boy, having been told about that, and the puppet shows and other delights besides, begged and pleaded with his mama to be allowed to see them. As nobody knew how long the ice would last, there was an extra note of urgency in his plea. Fortunately, his nurse was more than happy to take him, and so the treat was agreed for the following afternoon.

The nurse, however, privately informed her man friend of this jaunt, and so he was there at Blackfriars to meet their carriage. And the afternoon at the fair, with his company too, became an altogther different kind of day out. The little boy had his pleasures, including going on one or two somewhat unsuitable rides. But the adults also wanted to have their fun, of course. And it being cold, there were cups of hot spiced wines and ciders to be had, and brandy for the gentlemen, as well as porter and other drinks, which the nurse and her friend participated in with great gusto,

and increasing jollity, trailing the little boy behind as they visited the various stalls. At some point, having long since forgotten to hold firmly onto his hand, the nurse suddenly realised that her young charge, bored and ignored, had wandered away.

Now, of course, there was an outcry, but search as they would he could not be found. Gypsies were suspected, but nothing could be proved. The nurse of course, was sacked, but that didn't bring the little boy back. Mr and Mrs Montague, with all the money they had at their disposal, had the whole of London combed for their son, to no avail. Their dreadful distress was beyond all description, and Mrs Montague went from being one of London society's most envied women to being one of the most pitied.

Whether it was gypsies or others who had picked up the child, his smart clothes were soon sold, and he himself was cared for until he was old enough to be worth selling on, too. Being small and lithe, with, they claimed, 'a good head for heights', which was true in so far as he loved climbing trees, he was taken on by a chimney sweep who needed a boy.

Now, as the king's own grandfather had declared, when saved from a nasty fall by a sweep who soothed his startled horse, 'Chimney Sweeps should be regarded as Lucky!' And the Montagues' son was lucky, because he happened to get a master who was kind to him. But he was not at all fortunate to have a job as a chimney sweep's climbing boy, for it was horrible hard and dark work for anyone to be crawling through the chimneys of great houses in order to ensure that they were cleaned. However, perhaps because the chimney sweep took care of him, he survived.

And perhaps because the chimney sweep was a pleasant fellow, they worked in many of London's best houses. So it was that when the boy was nearly eight years old, they happened to be cleaning the chimneys in the house on the corner of Portman Square. These chimneys were large, and extensive. The young boy grew tired. Climbing down one of the smaller flues he found himself in a beautiful little bedroom. The bed in the corner looked so inviting, he could not resist going up to it. Sitting on the bed was a small cloth doll dressed like a tiny soldier. There was something about it that was so familiar, the little boy could not resist climbing onto the bed to take it in his arms. And the bed was so soft and the doll so comforting that he fell fast asleep.

When the sweep's boy did not re-emerge from the chimney, there was a search for him. He was not in any of the main rooms. The housemaids went upstairs and looked in the guest bedrooms, and the master and mistress' room too, but still they found no one. There was only one room they had not visited, but they were reluctant to look in there. For that was the bedroom of the Montagues' little son, who had been lost all those years ago. And on Mrs Montague's orders, the room had been left exactly as it was on that fateful day.

In the end they asked the mistress herself if she would mind checking that last chimney. It was Mrs Montague, therefore, who found the little sweep, fast asleep with the doll in his arms. She cried out in shock to see a child there, and he stirred, and opened his eyes. He was dirty, he was different, but she knew in that moment that he was her son returned. A little birthmark on his back soon had this confirmed.

You cannot imagine the joy in that house. Or the gratitude poured on the old chimney sweep for sparing his stick on that child. The boy was sorry to say goodbye to him, and made him promise to come and visit. Which he readily agreed to do, since he wouldn't be working so much anymore. Not now the Montagues had given him the reward they insisted he should have! From then on, the only work he'd be doing was weddings. A lucky sweep indeed!

And from then on, too, Mrs Montague had a personal concern for London chimney sweeps and for climbing boys especially. For the rest of her life she opened her doors every year to all the sweeps of London town, for a May Day luncheon feast. And every single one of them was treated to roast beef, plum pudding, and porter, with a shilling or sixpence apiece to take home after. And since it had become such a tradition, and chimney sweeps are ones to keep good traditions going, it went on long after Mrs Montague was gone. Even today, the doors of that house are often open to all. But maybe that's because it is now part of the British Museum.

21

WONDERFUL WIFE

There was a lad who lived round Cripplegate way, and he was courting. At least he hoped it might turn out that way before too long. They had talked, several times, and he was sure she also felt there was something special sparking between them. The trouble was, he was poor. He didn't have two shillings to rub together. And the girl – well she deserved something more. Not that she was a toff. But she was nice. Brought up right. And he was – well, if anybody asked, he liked to say that he was on his way to learning the shoemaking trade.

In fact, he was nowhere near that. He was absolutely at the bottom of the heap. He was one of the ones who helped the leather to tan. Not a very salubrious process because they used faeces for that, any they could get, but usually the dirt that the street dogs left. He'd be sent out with a bucket to pick up what he could. So as you could imagine, he didn't smell too good, although he was quite particular about having a good scrub whenever he got the chance. For he was a good lad at heart, and honest as the day is long. People said he was stupid that way.

Like the time when he heard a chink as he was running down the street and, turning round, he found a silver sovereign on the ground. What luck! But it was just behind a gentleman who had stopped to buy a paper, and it flashed through the lad's mind that maybe he'd pulled the sovereign out by mistake, when he put his hand in his wallet to pay. So without thinking twice, he picked up the coin and said, 'Sir, does this belong to you?'

The gentleman was amazed. But when he checked his pocket he was so pleased with the young fellow, you wouldn't believe. 'You've restored my faith in human nature,' said he. 'I'm delighted to meet a young man like you. Where are you from youngster, and what is it you do?'

Well, the lad started to stammer something about working for a shoemaker, but the gentleman was looking at him so intently he found himself slipping into the truth. 'Well Sir,' he explained, 'that is to say, I help with shoes in a way, for I'm a tanner's bucket boy. But I pretend I'm in the trade, 'cause I wish I could learn how shoes are made – and anyone can dream, can't they?'

'They can indeed,' said the gentleman, 'and sometimes dreams come true. I've a cousin who makes shoes, good ones too. I'll see if he needs an apprentice, an honest boy like you. Meet me here this time tomorrow, and I'll let you know.' And with that, and a tip of his hat, he was off and away down the street.

Well first the lad was so excited he was walking on air. Then he couldn't believe it at all; tomorrow the man wouldn't even be there. Of course it was only a gentleman's joke, he thought, as he waited next morning. But just as he was giving up hope, the man came round the corner. 'I'm sorry I'm late, but it's all arranged,' he called out with a cheery wave. 'As for apprentice fees, let me pay them now, please. You're honest enough to trust. Pay me back when you start to trade.'

So that was the start of a whole new life, and the young lad worked like a fiend. He was determined to be the best 'bespoke shoemaker' you could find. His fingers were nimble, and his eye was very good, and he was so eager to learn, he did everything he should. At the end of his seven years he was an absolute master. He could do a stitch so very small he did sixty-four to the inch. And he sewed at such speed if there was need for it, no one could work any faster.

The old gentleman, who'd often pop by to visit his cousin, was delighted with his protégée. Once he'd finished his apprenticeship, he paid the lad's freeman fees. 'Just so you can trade,' he said. 'I look after my investments.'

Now he was a shoemaker, and a freeman of London town, he had the skills to make good shoes, and the right to sell them too. A fine future lay ahead. And there was still only one person he wanted to share it with. Whilst he was an apprentice he had

been busy most of the time, but that young girl he wanted to court had always been on his mind. And he wasn't just seeing her in his imagination, because once he knew he was all set for a real profession, and he'd scrubbed off the lingering stink of his old one, he'd summoned up courage to ask her out. He'd been right about that spark, she'd said 'Yes' at once. So he and she had been walking and talking – and so on – ever since.

Where they went depended on when he was free, as he worked all hours. If it was dark, they'd go down by the river, watching the stars gleam on the water. If it was early, in the summer, their favourite place was Golden Lane. The goldsmiths would be working late on tables just outside their shops, taking advantage of the evening light. He'd admire the way they worked; the detail. She'd admire the work they'd done; the design. And they both enjoyed the sparkle. Secretly he also took note of the kind of rings she looked at most, promising himself he'd get her the best one day.

So he started saving a bit from every job he did, putting it aside for that ring. The trouble was, although he had the skills and the rights to do good business, he didn't have the money or the place to start one. All he could do was work for other people, which was alright to get by, but no way to let him buy. Not the ring he wanted anyway.

And the next thing was, when they were out one day, they both of them got a bit carried away, and he popped the question and she said 'Yes!' straight away, like before. So they were to be married, and now he just had to get the best ring he could afford. Which turned out to be the thinnest of gold bands. He only hoped that she would understand. Being the kind of girl she was, she did. When the day came and he slipped it on her finger, she said it was the loveliest ring she had ever seen. She meant it too. He knew that, but it made him all the more determined to give her a ring anyone would be proud of, when he could.

Fortunately luck was on his side. So was the old gentleman. Since his cousin was getting old, and not wanting to work much longer, he persuaded him to take on his apprentice as a partner. So now that lad had half a shop and all the work that he could want. Then he was earning money alright. Before long, enough to buy that ring. The sparkliest one you'd ever seen. Thick gold with a diamond on it. She loved it, but you know what? She kept her little band as well, wouldn't take it off.

Next thing he had to buy was a little house. Just in time before the baby came. It was right near St Giles-without-Cripplegate, which was handy for the christening. And for the next one too. Lucky the little house had a spare room. And space in the garden if they needed some more. Which was fortunate because she ended up having four. But his shoes and boots were in such high demand by then that money was no longer a real problem. Business was booming and he'd paid all his debts. As he got older he settled into being a man of wealth. Although he was generous with it too, helping other youngsters as he'd been helped himself.

He never complained about doing so much work. The only thing he minded was that now he had to travel a lot. People all over England, and Europe too, wanted to hear what he had to say about handmade shoes. For now there was competition from machines. That was why he was not there when his wife fell ill. They thought she had just fainted, but they couldn't bring her round. Her breathing grew shallower, and she simply slipped away. Of course they called the doctor, and he came at once. But her heart had stopped, and there was no pulse. There was nothing he could do.

When her husband returned and found she was dead he nearly went out of his mind. He couldn't forgive himself for being away; perhaps if he'd been there she might have been saved. He walked like a corpse himself with the cortege, and although it was only a step to the church, he had to be helped. Afterwards the children went to a neighbour's house, and he went home by himself.

It was all so sudden, the grave was not dug, so the coffin was laid in the crypt for the night. Rest In Peace she should have had then. But the sexton had noticed her diamond wedding ring. It had sparkled so, before the coffin closed, and it glittered in his head as he went back home. It was worth such a lot, and she didn't need it now. No one would know anyhow.

So, he crept back that night with a candle and the keys, and a knife in case of need. He unlocked the doors and went down into the crypt, and prised open the coffin lid. There she lay, arms crossed, and the candlelight caught an answering shine from the stone. What a waste it would have been to consign it to the dark. A diamond so large and hard against his palm.

Her finger was cold, and although it was bent, he managed to ease the ring free. He slipped it in his purse and reached to shut the lid. Then he saw the glint of another ring too, gold and lonely left behind. Waste not want not. He'd have that as well. He reached out again, to repeat his success.

But this little ring seemed to be held fast; he could get it to the knuckle but he couldn't get it past. He pulled and he twisted. The ring wouldn't move. But he refused to give up. If the finger wouldn't straighten it would have to be cut. So he took out the knife, and he sawed and he sliced at the finger of the lady in the coffin. And she, lying there, felt a searing pain that cut through the cold, and cut through the coma, and cut through the numbness that had held her like a corpse. She screamed herself awake and up in her box, and her eyes wide open too.

And the sexton, seeing this avenging ghost, dropped her hand and fled. No time to take the candle, nor to lock the crypt, nor to spare a second glance and see her rising to her feet.

Dazed and confused but joyously alive, she let the candle light her up and out, and home to her husband. That thin little golden band he'd bought had brought them together again.

They say in their second lease of married life, she had four more children before she died, and returned to be buried in St Giles.

22

Tea-leaves, Oysters and Shysters

As I was a-walking along a London street,
A pretty little oyster girl I chanced for to meet,
I looked into her basket, full boldly I did peep,
For to see if she'd got any oysters.

'Oysters, O oysters, O oysters,' said she,
'They are the finest oysters that ever you did see.
I sell them three a penny, but I'll give them to you free
For I see you are a lover of oysters.'

'Landlord, O landlord, O landlord,' said I,
'Do you have a little room that is empty and nearby,
Where me and my pretty little oyster girl can lie
While we bargain for our basket of oysters?'

We hadn't been upstairs for half an hour or more
When that pretty little oyster girl she's off and out the door,
She's gone and picked my pocket and down the stairs she tore
But she left me with her basket of oysters.

'Landlord, O landlord, O landlord,' I cried,
'Did you see the little oyster girl who was drinking by my side?
She's gone and picked my pocket!' But the landlord he replied,
'Son, you shouldn't be so fond of your oysters!'

One thing you're bound to be warned about in London – 'Tea-leaves'. Or – if you prefer to talk proper – 'thieves'. Dregs of society, but all part of the brew. And if the well-to-do are flush, the ne'er-do-wells will profit too.

So no time seemed better for the economic growth of both than when Victoria was young. Fresh on the throne – a brown haired, bright-eyed girl with a little bun under her crown. You can see it on the old 'bun pennies' if you're lucky enough to find one, and shine it up clean. Hopes were shining too, back in her day. And hopeful lads were hopping to it, out and about and learning all sorts of skills.

Down Smithfield way, businesses of all kinds was booming. Costermongers called out their wares: fish 'wet and dry', poultry, game, cheese, vegetables, fruit, flowers, and roots. Sellers of ready-to-eat treats drew customers by the nose for spice cakes and sweetmeats, hot eels and pickled whelks, sheep's trotters, penny pies, plum 'duff' and muffins, crumpets, brandy balls, and cough drops. Flying stationers, or running patterers, jostled for space with long-song sellers. And in and out of them all, ever-present and never noticed, silent as shadows, slipped the 'never sweats', the cadgers, cutpurses, prigs, petty pilferers, pickpockets. Plenty of names for different shades of the same game.

Mind you, they'd always been active in that area. Way back, when the River Fleet still flowed through it swift and sweet, it was handy for boats bringing goods and business through – and whisking away anyone who needed to slide out of sight nice and quick. But it had long since slowed into sludge and then a sewer, so solid with dead dogs you could skip across them like stepping stones. 'Fleet ditch' it was renamed then and Parliament called it a disgrace, and caused it to be arched over from Holborn to Fleet Bridge, or Ludgate Circus and Fleet Street as they became.

No doubt the noble gentlemen intended to cover up a multitude of sins. Instead, they simply helped them spread below. Because now there were so many splendid places to hide a hoard, or secret access points to drop through something 'hot' into a waiting box that floated on to be retrieved by some accomplice just downstream. Meanwhile, the thief, left innocently empty-handed, could saunter on slowly, letting the Bow Street Runners catch him at last. 'Aint got nuffin guv,' he'd laugh, and breathless with rage and wasted effort they'd have to let him go. Even though they knew – and had witnesses too – if he wasn't caught red-handed, it couldn't be proved.

And then there were houses, cunningly constructed over the river, linking one street to another, with escape doors in panelled walls and stairs that turned pursuers onto themselves or round dark corners to end in murky waters. Altogether a thieves' dream den, but an adder's nest for everyone else. Worse still if you went down Shoe Lane – where almost all inhabitants ran barefoot – and onto Saffron Hill. No trace there in that foul air of the fine fragrance and rich life of the past.

But amongst the many living and hiding in that dark place, there were plenty who held their heads high. They prided themselves on their skill – the speed and ease and stealth with which they stole. And top of the bill was a lad of seventeen or so, who'd been there ever since he was five. Probably an orphan, like so many others found in the street, trying to survive. Lucky for him he was taken under a good thief's wing, and learnt so fast he was soon better than his master.

He was such an expert in the 'art', you'd never even know he had brushed past, or feel your pocket being touched. He could take a necklace from under a lady's cloak while bowing and opening the door of her coach. He'd get a tip for it too. Being good-looking helped, of course, but he knew exactly what to do. He knew how to behave with a touch of class: to tip his hat, and to dress smart, but not in a way that would mark him out. Nothing special to remember him by. Unless you counted his 'lucky piece' – a little pocket watch, the first he'd ever pinched. And he kept that hidden, close to his heart, hardly ever even took it out.

This lad didn't work his local area, of course. He was off over the other side of town. The west side – the best side. Strolling down the Strand, or Piccadilly, or sometimes even Regent Street, newly built and very fashionable amongst all the top nobs, so the pickings were classy though the venture more chancy.

That's where he was one evening in early winter, still warm enough, but a bit foggy too. Good weather for working as far as he was concerned. There was quite a tidy crowd, moving slowly too, on account of the new gas lights which were French or something, so they had to be admired.

He'd done alright, and thought he'd treat himself for once, knock off a bit early. Reaching into his waistcoat to check the time, he stopped, shocked. Something very wrong – his watch was gone. He couldn't quite believe it but there was no other explanation. The biter bit – his pocket had been picked. But who could have done it? He, of all people, should have felt them feeling for it.

He looked around, watching for the tell-tale signs only an insider would spot – nothing. Everyone seemed purposeful; all the men were paired up and looking to their ladies. Then suddenly, out the corner of his eye, he noticed her. So sly, a hand trailing behind, reaching out, casual as can be. A woman! Young, respectably dressed, demure – he watched her a while, just to be sure. Then he casually followed, keeping his distance until she seemed to guess something was up. Then he was almost running and so was she, round a corner and down a side street. By the time he got there she had vanished into thin air – or would have done if he hadn't known that alley, with its handy little cranny, with room enough for one. 'Gotcha!' he said. 'Like you got my watch.'

Of course she denied it, pretended to cry, showed him her empty bag – all the tricks. He had to laugh. 'Never sweat!' he said. 'You're one of us. And I'm impressed. You're one of the best. Almost as good as me.'

She looked him up and down and grinned, 'We'd make a good team.'

And they did. Well matched; a handsome pair. Dressed up right, mouth shut tight, they could blend in anywhere. They got on, too.

You know how it is, one thing leads to another. Started off partners; ended up lovers. Then he got all romantic. 'Let's do it right,' he said, 'let's get hitched.'

They'd money to blow, so it was the real thing. Church bells, coach and four, even a wedding ring. Brand new too! Just the way to go.

Nature being as she is, and time being as he is, it wasn't long after that happy event before the young wife was showing signs of another one on its way. Saffron Hill, of course, was celebrating all over again. For there was no doubt, with parents like that, their child would be the best thief out.

When the day came, the birth wasn't too bad. They got the best midwife that could be had, and soon the lucky couple had a lovely little son. He was pretty well perfect – strong and healthy, but there was just one thing wrong.

The baby's right hand was curled tight like a fist, and try as they might they couldn't make him open it. Well of course it was his working hand. It really did matter. How could he follow his father's trade if it didn't get any better?

They took him to the doctor, the bonesetter, the lot. They tried everything – wouldn't give up. The one thing no one could understand was that there was nothing wrong with the little boy's hand.

The specialists were baffled, and the parents were running out of hope – as well as cash. Thinking they might refresh one or the other, they decided to have an evening off, and went out on the town to a top London show.

The one that was the craze of fashionable society at the time was a scientific demonstration from a famous mesmerist, who was also a learned professor. It was said he'd discovered 'animal magnetism' – the secret impulses of the brain. He could hypnotise anyone in the audience; persuade them to do the oddest things. Wonderful watching for everyone else, particularly since he'd often practice on the most wealthy or prominent person present. It was even more fun than going to the operating theatre to see a doctor dissecting a dead man, or stitching a limb back on to a living one. Although, both entertainments, being so absorbing to Victorian audiences, were popular with the pickpockets too.

They were dressed in style for the mesmerist, mingling in with the high-class cognoscenti, a frock coat for the little boy too, although, of course, he was too small for a proper top hat. Perhaps that was why the mesmerist picked them out. Or perhaps it was the way the mother suddenly sat up and took notice when he started to talk about the real importance of his science.

'The inward drivings of the mind,' he declared, 'can affect the outer body. I can cure what a doctor cannot understand.'

Either way, in a matter of moments, the little boy was carried forward to the stage as a subject to be practised on. He sat perfectly possessed, watching the audience bright eyed, while the mesmerist tried to manipulate his clenched right hand, and force it to open. He was unable to do so, and everyone sighed in sympathy as the mother bowed her head in disappointment.

'Wait,' said the mesmerist, with a confident smile, and reaching into his coat he took out his pocket watch, a fine gold piece, with a long chain. It glittered in the gaslight, and caught the child's eye.

'Now we will work through the mind,' announced the mesmerist, as he started swinging the chain slowly backwards and forwards. Right, left, right, left. The boy began to follow its swaying, left, right, left, right, his head copying the movement.

'You are feeling sleepy,' said the mesmerist. 'Your eyes are heavy.'

The little boy still looked wide awake.

'Let your eyes close,' hissed the mesmerist.

The boy nodded. His eyes gleamed. Then suddenly he thrust his tight little right fist towards the dangling chain. Before anyone had time to blink he had opened his whole hand and snatched the watch. As he did, something dropped from his hold, released at last from his grasp.

It was the midwife's gold ring.

23

TOSHER'S TALE

They say wherever you are in London, you are never more than a grave's length away from a rat. It used to be black rats. They were more arboreal, liked a nice warehouse, and a bit of booze; sit on a barrel of wine, they would, and dip their tails down the bung holes. They loved it round the markets, especially Borough Market – all sorts of passageways underneath. But the brown rats took over, and they're much bigger, and breed faster too. That's the kind you're close to nowadays. They settled into Borough Market as well, but they liked it even better down the sewers, especially in the old days when they opened to the river.

They weren't the only ones who slipped down there. The toshers did too. They'd go down to pick up any valuables, washed up from the foreshore or dropped down the drains. Lost jewellery, cutlery, coins. If you knew where to look, you could make a lot of money. Then wash the stink off, and dress up smart, and they never had any trouble getting a woman, because everyone would want to snag a good money bringer.

Official sewers workers never liked the toshers, because they took what were the workers' perks. After 1840 it was illegal to go down there, and there was a £5 reward if you grassed up anyone. So they took quite a risk, and that's apart from the danger, because the tide could rise suddenly, and if they weren't quick they'd drown. Or else get trapped, which was just as bad, on account of all the rats. A lot of men died that way, picked clean, right to the bone. But there were ways to get round them, if you knew how. The first silver coin that a tosher found down there, well, that was a luck piece, a guard against drowning. And if he did die, his friends put it in his mouth, and then the rats wouldn't eat him – so they said.

But better than silver, if you were a good looker, was the top of the lot, the Queen Rat herself. Toshers knew that, but they kept it quiet. Only sometimes stories got passed on. And this one came to a lady called Liz, from her great-great-granddad Jerry. He was a foundling, raised in a tosher family. And he only told when he knew he was dying; otherwise it wouldn't have been safe.

All toshers knew that the Queen Rat was down there. She might be watching, and if she took a liking to you, she'd see you alright. But when she really took a shine, she'd listen to you talking to your mates, and find out exactly the kind of girl you fancied. Then she'd change her shape, when the time was right, and meet you 'by chance' when you were out and about. If you gave her a good night, she'd repay you with a long life; you'd be in the money too, and no more worries. It could even pass down in your family. Whoever inherits it gets eyes like the river; one is grey, the other blue.

But if you got these favours, you must never say a word. If you let the secret out then the luck goes arsy-versy. And if you didn't satisfy the Queen Rat that night, or upset her in some way, well heaven help you then, for luck would be reversed in the nastiest way.

Anyway, Jerry, he'd heard all that. He'd been working as a tosher since he was seven. Never thought about it though – too busy working or enjoying himself. He was fifteen, good-looking, fit, funny, and usually had money. And he had a steady girlfriend. Though right then she was in the family way, so wasn't up for going out much. Of course he understood, but sometimes it was rough.

This particular night everyone was out on the town – it might even have been St George's Day. So Jerry got leave to go with his mates – a night off. There was plenty of drinking, and dancing and so on, and then a girl sat beside him at the bar. He liked the look of her alright, and she had plenty of spirit. She started matching him drink for drink. And what's more, she seemed to have a bottomless pocket. He thought she might be a mudlark, out for the day, out for a lark; she was certainly game for anything. So the night wore on, and the drinks went down, and their conversation began to fairly fly. Come around midnight they all decided to go on to a party. There were plenty going on late.

So then they got dancing, and they went well together. He was a smooth mover, and so was she. But she was kind of teasing him, winding him up. He wasn't averse to that, only it was a little bit public. And she let him know that if he liked that kind of thing, maybe they could go where they wouldn't be disturbed, and where they wouldn't have people falling over them. 'Why not,' he said. He'd half-forgotten about his own girl by then, anyway she was a long way from his mind.

So the two of them slipped out, left his mates behind, and started walking along by the river. There was a little bit of lamplight at one part, and it caught her eyes as they walked past, and it was funny, he could have sworn that they shone red. You know the way an animal's eyes reflect light? But he told himself it must be the drink, and anyway, she cuddled up close, and he had better things to think about. Then she said she knew where there was a good rag factory, and there was an easy way in.

So he followed on and they got inside and there were bags of rags of all sorts, and she made them up into a real cosy bed. And it was dark and nice and they got down to business.

They were having a great time, he was up for it as much as she was, until all of a sudden she jumped right on top of him and she gave him such a bite! It wasn't a woman's love bite; it was like a rat bite, straight through and into his skin. It gave him a real shock, and before he knew what was what, he upped with his arm and he gave her a wallop. But by the time his arm came down, she was gone. He sat up, the blood running down, with a big hole in his shirt there, and he looked all around and couldn't see her. So he struck a light, and there above him was the biggest rat he ever saw in his life.

She was hanging there, and looking down, and in her mouth there was a bit of torn cloth from his shirt. She dropped it, then she said, 'tosher, you can have your luck. But you've got to pay me for it yet. And you won't be done for a long time.' Then she was gone. He was so frightened he went straight home. Of course he didn't tell his mates, didn't tell anyone. Just waited to see what was to come.

And he did alright for money out of it. But nothing else. All his love life went wrong from then on. His girl, she died in childbirth. And his second wife drowned. The bad luck went across to them, you see. But he had six children. And you know what? One had a blue eye and a grey. She had hearing good as a rat, and she could walk around at night without a light.

But Jerry never told her why. Never told anyone. Not until the day he died.

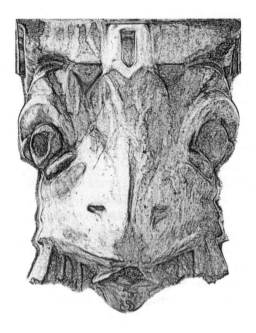

24

ROOM FOR ONE MORE

Many expectations changed in Queen Victoria's reign – even the view of a woman at the helm. After she had gone, these changes still went on, for women as well as men. Londoners looked to a wider, brighter world. Great Exhibitions influenced how people thought, how they looked at what they saw, what they might aspire to own, even how things could be bought.

Innovation opened commercial doors. Entrepreneurs like Selfridge created 'Department Stores'. That made London shopping in itself an end; you could just go and look and not even spend. Where else in the world would women's silk hats sit side-by-side with scientific advance? The display of Bleriot's monoplane was a masterstroke. No wonder people flocked to London town.

For some it was a long way to come. One young lady decided to break her journey by staying a night with friends along the way. They had a fine old manor house with plenty of room for visitors. Her bedroom was delightful, with windows opening to the front. But for some reason, perhaps because she was excited, she found it hard to sleep.

She was still awake at four o'clock, when she heard the sound of horse's hooves. Wheels crunched on the stones along the drive. Who on earth could be arriving so late at night? She looked out of the window and was shocked to see a black hearse driving up towards the house. Instead of a coffin, it seemed to be full of people.

It stopped just below her, and the driver stepped out. She saw his face quite clearly as he looked up at her. 'Room for one more,' he said, with a smile.

Terrified, she shrank away from the window, and when she looked again, the hearse had gone.

In the morning she realised it must have been a dream, though the sense of it clung to her for hours. But London, of course, proved the perfect antidote. Harrods was heavenly; Liberty liberating; and Oxford Street stimulating beyond all belief.

It was teatime before she noticed how exhausted she was. By then she had 'done the round' of the department stores. She was right at the top of one, on the fourth floor, but luckily it had a lift, which was a new thing in those days. That meant there might be a queue, but she was ready to wait. Five flights of stairs were more than she could take. Besides, a free lift ride was the icing on the cake. It even had a button to summon it up!

The lift arrived, and people poured out, replaced by a bigger wave rushing in.

It was so crowded now, she hesitated, and the lift attendant, seeing her, smiled. 'Room for one more,' he said.

His face was the same as the driver of the hearse. 'No,' she cried, backing away. He shrugged, and pulled the safety gates back across, then she heard the doors close, and the lift started to descend. Suddenly there was a scream, followed by an awful crash. The cable of the lift had snapped. Everyone inside it died.

25

GADGETS AND
GIRLFRIENDS

Lionel was one of those lucky young men whom fate seems to have
smiled on from the start. Well bred, well heeled, and well beloved
by male and female friends alike, he had sailed smoothly from
cosy cradle to comfortable career without so much as a hiccough
along the way. From his father he inherited a modest but solidly
established publishing business. From his mother he acquired a
drive to succeed and an instinct for opportunity. This, coupled
with his own good nose for modern innovation, and accurate
gauging of post-First World War sensibilities, had caused him
to back several new works which – against all expectation – had
turned out to be fashionable favourites and best-selling books. Still
relatively young, he was now the head of one of one of London's
most prestigious publishing houses.

His love of modernity extended to gadgets and machinery.
Instead of pen, paper, and messenger boys, he favoured the
typewriter and telephone. The ground floor of his office shook
with the smack and slide duet of fast fingers finding keys, and
typewriter carriages returning. The upper floors thrilled to the
clamour of telephone bells, swiftly intercepted by calm, clear-
speaking secretaries, who never confused the operator with
wrong numbers or letters, nor tried to talk into the earpiece.
And somehow, too, the girls knew if Lionel would want the call
redirected to his private line, up in his inner sanctum.

Despite his penchant for new styles and appliances, Lionel
had a sensible appreciation of traditional necessities for a decent
standard of London life. He was a member of a reputable
gentleman's club, and had a bachelor apartment in the best part of

Kensington. Here too, his staff were excellent, presided over by a butler of the 'old school', and Bowden, an indispensable personal valet. And although Lionel delighted in his stylish, if somewhat loud motorcar, he would frequently elect to walk to work or to visit a friend. He liked the exercise and it kept him trim.

Perhaps that was why, on a bright Sunday afternoon, having popped down to his office to check that a tiresome little job had been completed satisfactorily, he decided to leave his vehicle there, and stroll home slowly. Since it was such a promising day, he chose a very circuitous route, looping round and up to the green slopes of the western edge of London. He was already somewhat tired when he came to the wide spreading cemetery of Kensal Green, famous for its catacombs, and monuments in glorious Arcadian classical style. Particularly interesting too, from Lionel's point of view, was the burial place of the great Victorian engineer and innovator, Isambard Kingdom Brunel.

Determined though he was to see and appreciate this, the whole place was so enormous and sprawling he was feeling rather faint by the time he finished his sightseeing. Hurrying back towards the entrance lodge, without paying enough attention to where he was going, he soon found, to his rising panic, that he had lost his way. By now it was getting late. Perhaps it was near to closing time? Surely then someone soon would be making their rounds to ensure that everybody had left. He stood still and listened. Nothing. Although he wasn't squeamish, to be surrounded by the dead in this way was most unpleasant.

Setting off again, trying to retrace his steps, he determined to be more methodical in his search for the exit. Before long he came to a place that he thought he recognised, but on studying the graves he realised that they were more unkempt and uncared for than any he had seen so far. Then, at last, to his enormous relief, he saw a clear sign post stating the region that they were in: SWE 103. Well, he wasn't where he thought he was, but at least he now had some idea which direction to head in. Calmer now, he looked around for further clues.

Immediately beyond the notice were a few almost forgotten graves, one with carvings of roses upon the stone, but almost obliterated by ivy. Something about it caught his eye. Moving closer, he made out the words written on the stone. 'RIP Elsie …' he read – and then stopped. It was the name of a girl that he had known very well, in fact. She had been a girlfriend for a long time, off and on. He checked the birth date. It tallied. And the death? It was only a couple of years after he had last seen her. They hadn't exactly parted, just drifted apart – he couldn't quite remember why. He had been concentrating on work, getting ahead, his eyes fixed on higher things, and somehow she had been left behind. Extraordinary he hadn't even known that she had died. What a pity. She had been a sweet thing, good natured, with a lovely laugh. So full of life.

Now, as he looked again at her grave, he thought what a sorry state it was in. Was there no one who cared enough to clear the weeds and leave fresh flowers? Well at least that was something he could do. Resolving to pay for it to be cleaned up and restored to order, he went on his way. This time he found his way easily to the entrance, and met a cheery gatekeeper preparing to lock up.

'Oh Sir!' he said, 'Thought everyone was out already. Nearly here for the night you were! Still … peaceful place to sleep, alright!' Still smiling at his own joke, he hailed a hackney cab and helped

Lionel in. 'Look proper tired you do Sir, if you don't mind me saying. Good night!'

It was dark by the time Lionel got home, and it was only as he let himself in that he remembered it was Sunday. This was a day that he insisted his staff had an evening off. He liked having a bit of time entirely to himself.

Supper was laid out ready for him, as usual, and a welcoming fire in the grate. He poured himself a glass of wine, and picked at his food. But he didn't feel like eating. Nor being alone. Not tonight. He kept remembering Elsie. The way she walked; how she loved to dance; her eyes lighting up when he said something nice. How ready she always was to go out, or stay in, always agreeable to his whims. How quickly she'd turned away when he last said goodbye, having told her he'd be too busy to see her for a while – as if there was a sadness that she wanted to hide. Perhaps she had always cared more about him than he had for her?

He shook his head. No use sitting around and brooding. He had plenty of friends, usually more than he had time for. He'd invite someone round to share supper. Flicking through his address book he found a couple of possibilities – if one was out, another would be bound to be in. He picked up the telephone before he could change his mind, and asked the operator to connect him.

It rang a long time, and then there was a pause. 'Hello,' said a voice at last. It sounded rather distant. Perhaps they were standing too far from the mouthpiece.

'Hello,' said Lionel. 'Is that,' – he paused for a moment. Which was the number he had asked for? Which girl had he picked off the list?

'Hello,' whoever she was repeated, louder this time. 'Who is ringing? This is SWE 103.'

Lionel had already given his name before he stopped to think. Was that really the number he had asked for? There was something oddly familiar about it – and the voice too.

'Lionel?' The girl was clearly delighted. 'Is that really you, darling?'

This time, to his horror, Lionel thought he recognised it. And the number? Wasn't that the same as the signpost by Elsie's – no! It couldn't be.

'Sorry I took so long to answer!' she was saying. 'I was a long way away from the telephone. I've moved, you know. What about you?'

She sounded so normal. Somehow Lionel stuttered a reply.

'Still at the same place? Things must be going well then.' She laughed, and then stopped suddenly. 'But you don't sound … quite yourself. Are you alright, sweetie?'

Typical Elsie. Always sensitive to his moods.

'I'm … well,' he said, 'it's just – I … I …'

'Feeling a little lonely? Poor Lionel! Shall I come round? I'm not doing anything.'

He wanted to say no but instead, he mumbled something incoherent.

'Is that a yes?' He shook his head, but the words wouldn't come. 'Or a no?'

'No!' he cried. 'Not …'

'Not a no! Oh good,' she said. 'Then I'll be along as soon as I can.'

He heard her put the receiver down, but he himself could not move. Earpiece still clutched in his hand, he waited. A long time passed. Just as he was beginning to think it had all been a horrible nightmare, and had finally managed to get to his feet again, he heard a light step outside. Someone ran up the steps and tapped three times with the knocker. Three times swiftly and lightly. That had always been her special signal. He stumbled to the front door and pressed his ear against it.

'Lionel?' she said. 'Are you teasing me? I can hear you in there darling.' He saw his hand moving towards the handle of the door as if of its own accord.

Lionel's butler was, as usual, the soul of discretion, much to the annoyance of the downstairs servants, who were not aware of their master's unexpected seizure until after he had been taken to the hospital. Bowden, however, at least in the confines of his master's club, and then only to valets of a similar station, was more forthcoming. After all, it was he who had first discovered Lionel's body lying in the hall, on his return from his evening off. A dreadful sight to be met with.

'Particularly,' as he explained to his select group of listeners, because of the 'awful way young master's mouth was twisted. Lip lifted right up – like a scream frozen on his lips. Eyes staring from their sockets.' There'd been white marks on his face, too, which were oddly cold to the touch. 'But the strangest of all,' Bowden admitted, when pressed into further disclosures, 'was the clay. White clay. Don't sound much but it was smeared all over the carpet. And he was always so finicky about wiping his feet, wasn't he? But it couldn't have been anyone else. There were no footprints at all.'

To the astonishment of everyone who knew anything about the affair, Lionel did eventually more or less recover. But he was never like his former self. He seemed to have taken up the most unaccountable aversions. Particularly, God only knows why, he would never again use the telephone.

26

STREATHAM WIFE

If you're lucky enough to find true love once, you wouldn't expect to find it again. But Gertie did. Her second marriage was more of a companionship partnership to start with, she always said. But then it did grow into love. A different kind of love, perhaps, but just as strong.

Both he and she had been married before, and suffered the pain of loss; perhaps that was what had brought them together at first. But he had lost his first wife quite a long time before. Gertie had never known her. Apparently they had been childhood sweethearts. She had been buried nearby, at Streatham cemetery, and he still liked to go regularly and take flowers, or just visit her grave – really devoted.

But you can't always dwell on the past, and now they both had something to look forward to. After they got married, Gertie's new husband took her to Jersey. They liked it so much, it became their special place. But that first time, well it was a real honeymoon. And he bought her a lovely gold bracelet – a beautiful present.

When they came back, she let her flat go, and moved into his. It was a nice block, friendly and clean. He'd been living there for years. That's where he'd been with his first wife, too.

Anyway, by and by he wanted to go to the cemetery, and naturally this time Gertie went with him. But when she got back home, she realised she had lost her gold bracelet. She looked everywhere, checked her handbag and everything, but when she couldn't find it, she had to admit to him that it was lost.

'Ah,' he said. He had a bit of a funny look on his face. 'I think I know where it will be,' he said.

So he went out, back to the cemetery, and when he came home again he had the bracelet. He'd found it on his first wife's grave.

Well, Gertie didn't think much about it, because she wasn't a superstitious 'spooky' kind of person. And so she put it to the back of her mind and just got on with enjoying her new life.

But sadly that didn't last as long as they'd hoped, because after only a few years together he died. Well he had been a fair bit older than her; it was bound to happen, she said to herself. At least they had been happy for the time they did have together. She'd just have to get on with it.

So, as soon as she could face it, she decided to clear out the house for his sons. There were still a lot of things that had belonged to his first wife, too. Mostly Gertie had just left them in the cupboards while her husband was alive, but now she thought perhaps his sons would want them as well. So she started trying to sort everything out, and put it all into boxes.

But then things began to go wrong. It's a hard thing to do anyway, when you've lost someone, to have to go through all their possessions. But it was more than just that. It was odd. First one thing and then another seemed to crack as soon as she touched it. Then a cup slipped out of her hands altogether, and broke into smithereens on the floor. She couldn't think what was happening to her. As she always said, she wasn't a 'dropping things kind of person'. A soup dish, too – she knew it had been quite a special one for her husband – but as she was packing that into a box it shattered into shards.

Eventually she stopped – well she was getting a bit upset, naturally. So she decided to have a cup of tea. But as soon as she sat down with it, in an ordinary little chair, a solid enough piece of furniture, the legs slid out from under her and the tea went all over everything. Then even a spoon, a long spoon, she got hold of it and it snapped just like that.

Well, by now Gertie was really worried about what was the matter with her. She went outside to get a breath of air, and met a neighbour out in the courtyard. So they started chatting and before she knew it, Gertie had told her what was going on.

This other woman, she had lived there a long time. She listened, and then she asked straight away. 'All those things you dropped, did they belong to her, his first wife?'

'Come to think of it,' said Gertie, 'I suppose they did. Especially that soup dish; I think that might have been a wedding gift.'

'Ah well,' said the neighbour, 'that's it then. She just didn't want you to have her things. That's what. I suppose you knew they were childhood sweethearts? She was a bit of a jealous type. Everything had to be for her. I don't suppose she would have been pleased that he married again.'

'Well, there was no preventing that,' said Gertie. 'She was gone, and we met up. That's life.' But she couldn't help remembering what had happened to her bracelet.

'Good for you,' said her new friend. 'You made him happy. Do you want a hand packing up the rest of those things?'

The funny thing was, after Gertie had got rid of everything, it never happened again, there was no more bother. The first wife seemed to have gone. But though she had, Gertie always felt that her husband stayed on. And she wasn't the only one. For the vicar himself, when he came to visit after the funeral, told her that he was sure the spirit of her husband would always be in the flat while she was there.

And, as she said to me: 'I've lived there for a long time and I've never ever felt afraid there. I've had opportunity to move, but I like to be there. It just shows there are spirits. There's nothing more to say about it.'

27

SNAKES ALIVE
AND PUBS PAST

My friend D came to England when she was ten from Ceylon, as it was then, now Sri Lanka. Her family were living in London, Borough Market. It was bustling with business, but that wasn't such a shock because she was used to crowded colourful Columbo markets. Mangoes instead of apples, rice more likely than potatoes, but the same noisy selling spirit, goods piled in heaps, or laid out displayed, fingered by hawk-eyed customers, destined for the same end. The real difference was probably the weather, the wind whistling down the river, blasting up short skirts, instead of wafts of warmth stroking sarongs and silk saris.

There were some differences in livestock too. Chickens, dogs, cats and rats of all sorts on both islands, but the dazzling sweet salt fish of the Indian nation were a million miles away from a nice bit of pale plaice. D knew about that, because her father had come to England to bring tropical sea creatures and reptiles for display. His speciality was snakes, although he had problems flying them over after they escaped in the hold. So, occasionally he slipped some into his hand luggage, although that almost caused him trouble too. It was all because he was offered a meal, and thinking of his hungry pets he chose steak tartar, 'as rare as can be'.

'Ooh,' said the lady sitting next to him, 'I love really rare steaks, too.'

'Like my snake?' he said, assuming she was a kindred spirit, and opened up his bag.

It turned out she didn't like it at all, but fortunately by the time the air hostess responded to the loud screams, the snake was

safely stowed away in the luggage racks, the lady too incoherent to explain, and D's father all baffled innocence.

He simply didn't understand why there should be any difference perceived between reptiles and other lovely creatures. 'I'm just an exporter of Sri Lankan natural beauty,' he'd explain. This included, presumably, his daughter. Although D probably found the move smoother, and her charms were certainly more immediately appreciated in the new world and lifestyle of London. Especially when she went to college. But though her parents might have seemed unusual in some ways, there were other things that were the same as most Asian families in England then. An embargo on certain kinds of fun. For the daughters of the house at least, particularly if you were, like D, the only one. She couldn't go out with boys, like other girls did, or go to parties, and to make it worse she had to find excuses to save face.

Oddly enough the snakes helped her out in the end. For she met someone she liked, and he thought it was great that her dad kept snakes, because he had one himself! So D brought him home, and he and her dad looked in all the tanks and oohed and aahed about reptiles, and the boyfriend was established as the perfect young man. Even having a car now counted as a plus! He could drive her home much quicker than waiting for a bus.

And take them both on outings too. So what he and she used to do then, mainly at weekends, was to get together with some friends, and drive around, especially South London, discovering new pubs and clubs and out of the way venues to go to. He lived in Forest Hill, so quite often they'd start by heading out that direction, along the main road, Bromley or Eltham way maybe. It was all very leafy then, spacious too, and quiet after the city mayhem.

On this particular evening only one friend could come, a girlfriend of D's, and they were going roughly the Bromley route, although they'd turned off somewhere different from usual. They had been driving for a fair while, and both D and her friend needed to go to the loo, so they were watching out for somewhere they could stop. It was getting a bit dark, so they were looking quite hard, beginning to get a bit desperate, you know how it is. Finally they got to a Y junction, and then the boyfriend spotted a pub, so of course he pulled over, and they all piled out.

It was quite a grand place they'd found, one of those really old pubs, whitewashed, with big black beams. And they'd obviously gone to town on the old-style theme because they had lamps as well – great atmosphere. So the three of them went in and found what seemed to be the main bar. It was only then that they realised they must have walked into somebody's party, because everyone in there was wearing fancy dress.

Anyway, D's boyfriend went up to get some drinks and the two girls headed off to the toilet. There weren't any signs saying 'Ladies', but that wasn't as common then as it is now. So they just headed towards the back, looking for a likely door. They soon saw one, but when they went through they found themselves in a long back room. And it was absolutely full of hats! They were all along the walls, rows of them – hats of all sorts. There was a fur one with a tail hanging down that D rather fancied, and a lovely big one with a feather.

D and her friend went straight on through, because they were in a hurry to get to the loo. And by now they were beginning to feel rather embarrassed, because everyone here was also dressed up to the nines. One woman had a floor-length gown with all her hair done in ringlets. And two men were in total cavalier style, with flowing sleeves and high boots and everything. It was really glorious to see, but poor D and her friend were just in jeans and t-shirts. They wished they'd known in advance!

At least they'd spotted another door which had to be the toilet because it was very small, so they pushed that open with a sigh of relief and hurried in. Only it wasn't what they were expecting at all. It was more a sort of corridor which seemed to be running in both directions but it was hard to see because it was so dark. There were two of the lantern-type lamps, one on either side, but they obviously had faulty bulbs or something because they were flickering really badly.

At this point D and her friend looked at each other, and agreed they'd had enough, and maybe they didn't need the toilet all that much! It was just too dark and odd to go on – almost spooky. So they backtracked quickly.

D was ahead, and just as she got to the door a gentleman appeared – and he really was a gentleman, because he opened the door for her with a real flourish and a bow! She noticed the lace flutter at his wrist as he moved. He was obviously well practised at it. And he was very good looking too. So, while she was taking all this in, and enjoying being back into the light again, she forgot all about her poor friend. And so did the dashing gentleman, apparently, because far from giving her the same treatment too, he slammed the door right in her face! She was shut out in the dark and naturally felt most put out. 'It's bad enough that you are prettier than I am,' she said when she caught up with D again, 'but honestly, he treated me as if I was completely invisible! I don't think I like this place at all!'

Anyway, they went back into the bar, and there was D's boyfriend looking rather pleased with himself, with three drinks in front of him. 'We should tell everyone about this place,' he said, 'because they wouldn't take my money when I tried to buy a drink.'

'There you are,' said D's friend. 'It must be a private party. I don't think we should stay. No one's talking to us anyway.' It was true, although D hadn't noticed until then. It wasn't that everyone was being rude. It was just that they obviously didn't really belong to that crowd. So they drank up quickly and left.

But of course, when they got back and told their friends, everyone wanted to go to this place where the drinks might be free, and the people were wonderfully weird. So they all drove out the following week, ready to make a night of it. This time they were all dressed up as well. D's boyfriend was driving, obviously, and D and her friend were helping to direct him, and they got to the place where they thought they'd stopped before, but there was no building there. So they drove up and down, and looked around, and they ended up back in the same spot again. 'I really thought it was here,' D's boyfriend said, but he didn't seem so sure any more. It was just after a Y junction, but there was nothing there, only the road and a space on the side. And fields and trees, of course, but not a single building.

Naturally their friends assumed it was a trick, and not a very funny one either, since they were the ones who'd been fooled. And since they were all dressed up now, they made D and her boyfriend take them to a pub on the way back, and pay for everyone's drinks too. And they were stared at by everyone in there for wearing fancy dress. It was a bit of a difficult evening all round. By the end of it, if there hadn't been three of them who'd seen it, even D would have thought she'd imagined it all.

It took a long time to live it down. If ever one of them happened to say, 'Let's go somewhere new,' someone would be bound to bring it up again. 'Oh yes, do let's – how about that pub that wasn't even there?'

Anyway, time passed. They finished at college. D and her boyfriend split up, and more or less lost touch. And that might have been the end of the story. But many, many years later when D was working, she was looking for a school not far from Bromley. Only she got lost. She was driving along – you know the way you do, hoping you'll just find yourself by pure fluke – when she came to a place that somehow seemed familiar. It was a Y junction, and just past it was a space like an unofficial lay-by. Down beyond that was a petrol station, so she pulled in there to ask the way. It was an old man serving at the counter, and she told him that she was lost, and he was very helpful and gave her easy directions to the school. Then, just as she was going – it was an afterthought really

– she asked him about the open area up the road. 'Wasn't there a building once, a sort of pub just there?'

'Oh,' he said. 'I'm surprised you know. I thought you said you weren't familiar with this area? There did used to be a pub there. Well it was a coaching inn really. Very old it was, maybe seventeenth century or so. I'm only going on what I was told, mind. I never saw it myself. They say that it burnt down 200 years ago.'

'I know it sounds funny,' D said to me. 'It's hard to believe it myself. But I know what I saw. And remember, I didn't grow up here. I don't know much about history and what people wore. I knew even less back then. So how could I dream it all up and yet get all the details right? And how could three of us dream the same thing all on the same night?'

28

BIKE HIKERS

Standing at the bus stop outside Bromley-by-Bow tube station, just up from the Blackwall Tunnel, freezing cold wind blowing one way, and the blast of exhausts from traffic thundering past the other, I counted every kind of lorry I'd ever seen, apparently all heading for Stratford, but not a bus amongst them.

Meanwhile, the bus queue had been growing steadily longer ever since I'd arrived, and I was asking anxiously if it was the right stop. Most of the people there were old timers, knew all the routes, and were ready to take me under their wing. 'They are like birds of a feather, buses are,' said one man to nobody in particular but with an eye on me because I seemed most interested in chatting.

'Why is that?' I asked, happy to hear the same old joke. 'Because they always stick together,' he says, and everyone nods and begins to complain all at once.

'I saw four together last week,' claimed one woman with a pram.

We go on waiting. The line gets longer, 'I only want to get to Stratford; maybe I should try hitching.'

'You don't want to do that,' the queue agrees. 'They'd knock you down soon as stop.'

'It's not safe now, for a woman anyway,' the old man added.

'Not for a young man, neither,' says a lad, who has been pretending he wasn't listening.

'Really?' Several people look hopeful. 'We've been standing around for a long time, and we could all do with a story, preferably gory.'

'Well, my friend,' he hesitated, obviously a scrupulously honest young man. 'Well he's a friend of a friend, really,' he admitted. 'But

I've met him and I know it's true. He is a biker, lives in Stratford, but thinks nothing of popping up to Scotland, or down to Brighton or somewhere just for a cup of tea. Him and his girlfriend they're always off; they go everywhere. But this time, he'd just gone down to Blackheath to see a mate, he was on his own. It was quite a while back, maybe even twenty years ago. Anyway, he was on his way back home, late afternoon, and he saw someone standing next to a lay-by with a sign on a bit of card saying "Stratford please". Young bloke, didn't look like he was a lorry driver, broken down or anything, and you don't usually get people hitching in London do you?'

'So anyway it caught my friend's eye, and I suppose he was a bit surprised so he'd slowed right down, and then, because the bloke was looking after him, he stopped. And he asked him where exactly he was going, and it was some address in Stratford which my friend knew, so he said he could give him a lift all the way home if he'd be up for a ride on the back of a motorbike. My friend had his girlfriend's helmet with him, you see, in the box on the back.'

'Well, the bloke was delighted. "Yes please," he said. "I'm used to motorbikes, anyway, although I'm usually riding in front. But I did go pillion once." So he put on the helmet – bit small but it was just about alright – and hopped on the back and off they went.'

'Well, my friend went a bit easy at first, because, although he was used to having someone ride pillion behind him, you always have to adjust balance with each new person, depending on weight. But this bloke was very light, and didn't wriggle about, so there was no problem, and my friend could more or less forget about him and concentrate on the road. Which he really had to do then because there were a lot of new speed limits on that bit of the road, and you had to keep an eye out for police cars. But anyway, it wasn't that long before they came up to the Blackwall Tunnel and the bloke on the back shouted something about them having made good time. It was about teatime by then, I suppose. But it was really getting busy. So, when they went into the tunnel, my friend just kept a steady pace, sticking on the inside lane, concentrating. Some drivers are so crazy in there, you have to watch out in you are on a bike.'

'When he came out on the other side, it had started to drizzle. Funny that isn't it? It can sometimes be a different kind of weather on one side from the other. So anyway, he just half-glanced over his shoulder to see if the other bloke was alright and blow me! He got such a fright! He couldn't see anyone there.'

'So as soon as he could, of course, he pulled off and it was true. There was no one on the back. The poor bloke must have fallen off! Well you can imagine how my friend felt; he was gutted and couldn't think what to do at first. No mobiles then you see. It's hard to remember how we managed without them! But anyway, of course he had to. He thought he'd go on to one of those emergency phones that they had by the side of the road, but the last one he'd passed was quite a way back'.

'So then he decided it would probably be quicker if he went back himself to try and see what had happened. But, of course, he couldn't just turn around. He had to get off the northbound road and over onto the southbound approach and back through the tunnel. And then, of course, cross over again, and head back up northwards the way he'd just come.'

'It was all a bit of palaver and the traffic was getting worse, moment by moment, and of course my friend was beside himself worrying about this bloke. But there was no sign of an accident when he finally approached that northbound bit of the tunnel again, and he was trying to hope that was a good sign.'

'This time, going through, he really crawled along on the inside line again, and he was driving that slow, he ended up with a line of bikers stuck behind him. And they started hooting, and when he still didn't get a move on at all, they were all shouting and trying to overtake and all that.'

'But my friend just kept on as he was, trying to stay calm, and shining his light as best he could to the wall side, to see if there was anyone lying there, or even just a scarf or something that might have blown off. Or anything at all. But there was absolutely nothing. Which in a way was a relief but on the other hand, it was completely impossible.'

'When he got through he pulled off at the first transport café he passed and had a cup of tea with three sugars just to steady himself. Then he started to think maybe he was going mad and he'd just imagined it all. So he went back out to the bike to see if his girlfriend's helmet was there. But it wasn't, and the way it was fixed on there was no way it could have fallen off by itself.'

'He went on home in a bit of a daze and it was only when he saw the signs to Stratford that he remembered the guy he had given a lift to had been going to Stratford as well, and he'd even mentioned an address, which rang a bell. My friend had to rack his brains, but then it came back to him. So, of course, he went straight there.'

'It was a little semi-detached house. Quite nice. Nothing odd about it at all. So he went up and rang the bell, but there was no answer. He was just about to go when he thought he heard a sound from inside the house, and then out of the corner of his eye he caught somebody twitching a curtain back. Well, maybe whoever it was might not want to open the door to a stranger, but by then there was no stopping him, he just had to speak to somebody, and normal behaviour didn't seem to matter anymore. So he leant on the bell until he heard them coming, and the moment the door started to open he jammed the end of his boot into the crack, and began trying to explain why he was there. Then he saw a woman looking out at him, and he stopped. Because, although she must've been in her fifties or so, and she had clearly seen better days, there was something about her face – her eyes, mostly – that my friend said were the dead-spit likeness of that bloke who'd been on his bike.'

'"I'm sorry," he said, and it all came tumbling out in a rush and as soon as he said "Blackwall Tunnel", it was like a light bulb went on in the woman's head. She flung open the door and caught hold of my friend by the arm.'

'"Did this boy look like me?" And almost before she heard the answer she started to cry.'

'Well, of course my friend felt awful. He didn't know what to say or how to comfort her, because he still didn't have a clue what was going on. But after a while she calmed down a bit. "You'd better come in," she said. They went into the kitchen, and she even made some tea. And then she told him.'

'Apparently her son had been at a party at Blackheath somewhere. Sort of thing that goes on all night and a bit into the next morning too. So anyway he was ready to come home around lunchtime; he'd even phoned to say when he'd be back. But there was another Stratford lad at the party who was going to hitch home, and he'd already set off quite a bit earlier, but he hadn't had any luck at all getting a lift, even though he'd made himself a sign and everything. So this woman's son had stopped when he saw his mate still sitting by the side of the road, and had offered him a lift. The problem was that the friend was a really bad passenger: he kept on leaning the wrong way, nearly having them over. "So somehow or other," the woman said, "he persuaded my son to swap over, and let him drive – you know, be at the front, and my son went behind him. Damn stupid thing to do, but maybe they had done it before, I don't know. And of course there was only one helmet. You didn't have to wear one then, you know, but my son always did when he drove, because I'd always insisted on it. So he handed over the helmet to his friend. And they got on alright until they got to the Blackwall Tunnel. But about halfway through that, there was an accident. The other boy survived."

'But her son hadn't. He'd been killed outright. At 4:25 p.m., the police report had said, apparently. Exactly the same time as my friend was passing through the tunnel.'

'"It was ten years ago," the woman said. "Ten years ago today. That's why I'm here at home and not at work. Although I usually don't open the door to anyone."'

'Well, my friend stayed as long as he could, and listened to her talking about her son. And drank his cold tea. He felt it was the least that he could do. She told him the cemetery where her son was buried too. And he promised he would stop by to pay his respects. Then he went. He'd had enough. He just wanted to get away, and to try to forget about the whole thing. He was really shaken up about it. But somehow he couldn't let himself go past the cemetery without having a look. He'd promised, and he kind of felt he owed it to the young lad too.'

'It was quite a big cemetery and hard to find the grave. But when he did, he was in for another shock. Hanging on the headstone was his girlfriend's helmet.'

29

SECRET COOKING POT

We were in Southwark, swapping stories – tales of coming to London, too. Some had come there in the 1950s and '60s from the Caribbean, others a little later from Africa.

'It was hard,' one woman said. 'The food – oh! We couldn't get things from back home, like you can now. It was different then! But I had a friend, she was from Jamaica too. We worked at the hospital. I came as a trained nurse, you know. And we lived in a hostel. Mmmm! Somewhere to sleep, but no kitchen or any place to cook. So, what we did was, we cooked at night in our room, with some of the other girls. We had a little stove. Big trouble if we'd been caught! But that's what we did. But we couldn't always wash the cooking pot, because we only had the bathroom. We were afraid someone would see us! But it added to the taste! Yes, it all got sunk into the pot.'

'That's like the story of the magic cooking pot,' I said. 'It loses its power if it gets washed.' 'Isn't it an Anansi story?'
'Ananse's from Ghana!' someone exclaimed.
'Jamaica too,' another added.

So we tell the story between us all. How there is hunger all around, and everybody tightening their belts and chewing their cheeks. But Anansi finds a magic pot that cooks by itself, and fills up with food. All Anansi has to do is say the words. And remember never to wash the pot. Easy – Anansi is lazy. And greedy. He keeps the pot secret. But his wife sees he's getting fat when they're getting thinner. She follows him, and she sees and she hears the words too. So next day she uses the pot and everybody eats. But then she washes it. And all the magic is cleaned out.

London is like that pot. Layer upon layer of story going in – one on top of another. Each tastes different. Variety is the spice of life. Each adds to the others. Better and better the more it's mixed up … let's hope no one ever tries to clean it out!

NOTES

*Asterisks are used to refer readers to books in the Bibliography.

Introduction
Illustration: Stained-glass window, All Hallows by the Tower. Reproduced by permission of the vicar. Together with its Roman paved Undercrotft Museum, this wonderful church spans London through the ages.

'I saw' – adding mid-line semi-colons makes sights plausible. Illustration: Hobbs Barber, Borough Market.

Alba to Brutus (BC)
Story mixes giant lore, Geoffrey of Monmouth's *Historia Regum Britannia*, and Lord Mayor's account of Gog and Magog. London Stone was also said to be the milliarium, and heart of the city, where oaths were sworn, debts paid, and Lordship of the city claimed (e.g. Jack Cade). Illustration: Railings round London Stone, Cannon Street.

Bran the Blessed (BC)
From the Mabinogion – 2nd Branch. Bran's buried head was one of 'three fortunate concealments' in the Welsh triads. Illustration: 'Colin'. Steel sculpture by Luke Morgan (2009). Beneath Old Operating Theatre, Southwark.

Boudicca (AD 61)
Written for this collection by storyteller Xanthe Gresham; 'spirit' location details added by H.East from local oral beliefs

(Epping Forest/Waltham Forest Arts Project 2003), internet and archaeological paper on Kings Cross area excavation revealing Roman camp. Illustration: door detail Bank of England.

London Bridge (100–present day, Romans–Elizabeth II)
A string of stories, related to London Bridge and rhyme. Sources: oral – 'Southwark Storyswap'*; Lady Gomme regarding sacrifice/ fair lady link; Jon Lewis* regarding Olaf. Hay's Wharf Company's St Olaf House replaced church of St Olave (cf mural). Illustration Boss Badge of the Priory of St Mary Overie reproduced by kind permission of The Chapter of Southwark Cathedral

William I and Sons (1066–87)
Bird Story – tale type 920 B, retold from Briggs*. Illustration: Emblem St Olave's Court – 3 birds.

Rahere (1100–54, Henry I–Stephen and Matilda)
Sources: Leonard Clark's church pamphlet; Internet; George Worley's 'Short History'; translations of William of Nangis and William of Malmesbury (regarding the White Ship), 'No ship ever brought so much misery to England'. Rahere was close friends with Bishop Richard de Beaumis (probably I). Smithfield was then Smedfield or Smoothfield. Illustration: Priory church of St Bartholomew the Great, archway shield.

Witch Well (AD)
Rare specifically London folk tale with rhyme heard from Essex borders schoolgirl, learnt from her grandmother. Bagnigge was an old name for River Fleet.

Gilbert Becket's Crusade (1087–1135, William II–Henry I)
Sources: medieval legends 'without foundation in fact' including: the Golden Legend and 'Young Beckie' ballad; also Hugh (Pye) de Kopeck family tales. Local lore claims Becket's parents were married and buried at St Paul's. History agrees Gilbert was a mercer. Illustration: Mercer maiden, Mercer Hall, Ironmonger's Lane.

Thomas à Becket Legends (1154–89, Henry II)

Sources: Oral – Joan Cottle, Lambeth Palace guide. Written Golden Legend and others, York Minster and Canterbury Cathedral's stained-glass windows. Westwood and Simpson*. Grim's personal testimony. Internet (especially Rebecca Howard on pet starling miracle. Caught by kite it invoked St Thomas. Kite dropped dead!) Illustration: Becket birthplace marker, Cheapside.

Blind Beggar's Daughter (1272–1307, Edward I)

Source – pub lore. Briggs*. Thomas Percy (1765) added 'Henry, son of Simon de Montfort' twist to older ballad, 'The Beggars Daughter of Bednall Green'. I used earlier name, Bethen Hall, and avoided naming the son, because some did survive the baron's revolt and were pardoned by Edward.

Dick Whittington (327–1413, Edward III–Richard II–Henry IV–Henry V)

Much is legend, but Richard Whittington existed, was apprentice to Fitzwarin, and married his daughter, Alice. Thrice Lord Mayor of London, he left bequeaths and laws as described. Coal barge, Lea and Bow details from internet and historian Rosemary Taylor. Sites: Highgate Hill marker, Whittington Hospital. Illustration: Cat. Worshipful Company of Goldsmiths churchyard of St John Zachary.

Ghosts in Good Company (1483–present day, Richard III–Elizabeth II)

Oral source. Site: Tower of London. Illustration: Church of St Bartholomew the Great, shield.

St Uncumber's Shoes (1558–1603, Elizabeth I)

Expanded from brief reference in Briggs*. The condemned man's right to 'address the crowd' still exists as Speakers Corner, Hyde Park. St Uncumber's statue was lost with Old St Paul's in the Great Fire of London, but Westminster Abbey's bearded lady figure may be her. Inscribed stone commemorates public declarations at St Paul's until 1640s. Illustration: The Cross of St Paul's

The Inns Of Court (1558–1603, Elizabeth I)
Sources: O'Donnell* and Guildhall Library notes. Sites: Lincolns
Inn; the Temple (church of Knights Templar). 'Inns of Court
students are sons of persons of quality, those of inferior rank not
being able to bear the expenses.' Fortescue.

The Lambeth Pedlar (1558–1625, Elizabeth I–James I)
I interwove the (earlier) Swaffham folk tale and the church of
St Mary Lambeth legend (detailed in Briggs*) to make sense of
the storyline and character of the hero. Such a meeting of minds
might have happened … The original 1608 pedlar window was
replaced after Second World War bombing. Illustration: The
George Inn.

Rebecca and the Ring (1603–49, James I–Charles I)
'The Cruel Knight' ballad/legend became attached to Dame
Rebecca Berry because of fish and apparent ring on her
monument, St Dunstan and All Saints church (actually her second
husband, Elton's coat of arms). 'The Devil's Tavern' built 1543 was
notorious for smugglers. Rebuilt as 'The Prospect of Whitby' it is
one of London's oldest pubs. Illustrations: Billingsgate fish market,
weathervane and railings.

Light-Hearted Highwayman (1603–25, James I)
Source: Alison Barnes* and oral (Epping Forest Project, 2003)
Tyburn was the boundary stream; executions took place from
1196–1783; Tyburn (Triple) Tree was built 1571 allowing many
to 'Go West' to 'dance the Tyburn Jig' simultaneously. Illustration:
Tyburn Marker, Marble Arch, Edgware Road.

The Lodger of Soho Square (1702–14, Anne)
Source: Westwood and Simpson*. Charles II's statue was removed,
but returned to Soho Square in 1938. Illustration: Priory church of
St Bartholomew the Great, archway shield Weave Well.

Becky of Bedlam (1760–1820, George III)

O'Donnell* and other sources; oral claims of sightings – Internet. Becky's ghost most recently reported 'looking for her sovereign' in Liverpool Street station, which stands on the site of St Mary of Bethlehem Priory, the original Bethlem Hospital. Part of Bedlam's specially built premises in St Georges Fields were used for the Imperial War Museum.

Lucky Sweep (1760–1820, George III)

Many sources; 1814 was the last frost fair, because London Bridge was rebuilt 1831 with wider arches, facilitating tidal flow. 'Sweeps are Lucky' saying ascribed to George II. Illustration: Dragon, emblem for City of London.

Wonderful Wife (1830–37, William IV)

Sources: Westwood and Simpson* and O'Donnell* who says the story was on woman's gravestone, parish church of St Giles-without-Cripplegate. This is now part of the Barbican; I've not found the gravestone (yet). Cobblers mend, shoemakers make shoes; '64 stitches to the inch' marked shoemakers' superior craftsmanship in battle against mechanisation. Illustration: Blacksmith Emblem, All Hallows by the Tower (by permission of the vicar).

Tea-leaves, Oysters and Shysters (1837–1901, Victoria)

Oyster-girl song – broadside ballad; I learnt this version from traveller Duncan Williamson. Story – London joke extended using Mayhew interview with young thieves. Thanks also to Old Operating Theatre (of Old St Thomas Hospital) and the Internet for details of Victorian operations and mesmerists, and Andrew Duncan's *Favourite London Walks* on Saffron Hill. Illustration: Smithfield market railing.

Tosher's Tale (1837–1901, Victoria)

Westwood and Simpson. My version has some details from Mayhew, but is mostly told fom oral source (Liz Thompson recorded for Southwark Storyswap – look out for her forthcoming book. Her Tosher relative grew up in the Snow fields and Borough riverside area). Illustration: Gutter creature, Talbot Lane.

Room for One More (1901–10, Edward VII)
Retold from Briggs*, Selfridges details etc. added. Illustration: Beehive, Gresham Street.

Gadgets and Old Girlfriends (1910–36, George V)
Retold from Roud*. Cemetery associated with ghosts – Cowdell (FLS) heard from someone who saw a knight in full armour nearby. Illustration: In Loving Memory, Kensal Green cemetery.

Streatham Wife (1952–present day, Elizabeth II)
Retold as remembered from Gertie (Southwark Storyswap). Illustration: Southwark Tavern, Borough Market.

Snakes Alive and Pubs Past (1952–present day, Elizabeth II)
Retold from oral source – Debbie Guneratne. Site Borough Market and Bromley. Illustration: Priory church of St Bartholomew the Great, archway shield.

Bike Hikers (1952–present day, Elizabeth II)
Source Westwood and Simpson*. Site Blackwall Tunnel.

Secret Cooking Pot (1952–present day, Elizabeth II)
Oral sources. Illustration: Old and New, Dragon and Plane, St Mary-le-Bow.

BIBLIOGRAPHY

Barnes, A., *Essex Eccentrics* (Boydell Press, 1975)

Briggs, K.M., *A Dictionary of British Folk Tales Volumes I & II* (Routledge, Kegan Paul, 1971; 1970)

East, H. & Corkery, K. *In Search of the Spirit of Southwark* Southwark Storyswap (Southwark Festival, 2000)

Lewis, J.E., *London the Autobiography* (Constable, 2010)

Mayhew, H., *London Labour and the London Poor* (1861)

O'Donnell, E., *Ghosts of London* (Philip Allan & Co. Ltd, 1932)

Roud, S., *London Lore* (Arrow Books, 2008)

Rutherfurd, E., *London* (Arrow Books, 1998)

Stow, J., *A Survey of London 1598* (The History Press, 2009)

Vale, G., *London Fairy Tales* (Pitman, 1949)

Westwood, J. & Simpson, J., *The Lore of the Land: A Guide to England's Legends, from Spring-heeled Jack to the Witches of Warboys* (Penguin Books, 2005)